—— **MY OLD** ——

KENTUCKY

ROAD TRIP

— MY OLD —
KENTUCKY
ROAD TRIP

HISTORIC DESTINATIONS & NATURAL WONDERS

CAMERON M. LUDWICK & BLAIR THOMAS HESS

PHOTOGRAPHY BY ELLIOTT HESS

THE
History
PRESS

Published by The History Press
Charleston, SC 29403
www.historypress.net

First published 2015

Manufactured in the United States

ISBN 978.1.62619.816.6

Library of Congress Control Number: 2014959984

To our fellow proud Kentuckians—young and old, native and transplant—who, like us, have not yet begun to explore the great Bluegrass State. We are honored to be your tour guides on this extraordinary journey.

And to our families, who planted their roots here and gave us the privilege to claim our birthright in the Commonwealth.

CONTENTS

CONTENTS

Introduction

WE'RE GOING ON AN OLD KENTUCKY ROAD TRIP

There's no rule that says you have to start your road trip at a particular beginning. In fact, when it comes to road trips, there really are very few rules at all. They require a delicate balance of organization, but not too much preparation, and a willingness to fly by the seat of your pants and understand that the most fun parts of your adventure will be the unplanned ones.

Like the time we saw a sign proudly declaring, "We sell cheap moccasins, y'all," and had to hit the pause button on our drive to Mammoth Cave National Park to pull into Leroy's Olde Gener'l Store. Yes, we spelled that right. Y'all can hardly ask two ladies to deny themselves a pair of cheap moccasins. As it would turn out, this detour allowed us to meet Leroy, a self-declared original American picker who opened his general store when his wife would no longer allow him to bring his "found treasures" into her house. She drew the line, and now Leroy draws a profit as locals and unsuspecting tourists find themselves curiously poking their heads into a store that is literally bursting at the seams—and spilling into its parking lot—with unique antiques, old jars and bottles, a surplus of Kentucky license plates hammered at the nearby state prison, a few taxidermied treasures, and even a shot glass proudly branded by the national park down the road.

Never mind that this stop meant we missed our park tour by fifteen minutes and had to wait half a day for another tour that had two open spots. The important thing to remember is that, in the end, we did get to see the inside of that amazing natural wonder—the cave, we mean, although Leroy's is most certainly a wonder in our eyes—and we did so in our brand-new, very affordable moccasins.

As any good road tripper knows, you're going to need a few key items before you head out:

A camera. We have a newly acquired, very fancy camera with more buttons than Kentucky has counties, and we're still figuring out the puzzling thing. So we also take along our trusty camera phones as backup, and sometimes, when we're feeling particularly nostalgic, we bring along an old film camera. Just grab something to help you capture a memory, to help you share what we're sure will be a grand adventure with your family, friends, and strangers who you're going to encourage to visit this place too. But take this piece of advice with you as well: Don't forget to be present. Take in your surroundings; experience the history and wonder of this fascinating state. Don't be so busy capturing memories that you forget to make one.

An idea of where you're headed. Now, this doesn't necessarily mean that you need a plan, and you definitely don't need a schedule. But if you set out on a Saturday and you have somewhere that you need to be by Monday morning, we'd recommend at least knowing what direction you're going to point the vehicle. It'll keep you from getting overwhelmed. And if your destination requires you to be at a certain place at a certain time for a tour or a show, make sure you plan accordingly. Plan on getting lost at least once. Plan on a pit stop for gas and snacks. Plan on a few bathroom breaks. Plan on at least one detour (e.g., cheap moccasins). Plan to have a backup plan.

A full tank of gas and a map. Directions are good. A GPS is even better. Neither one is always going to be reliable. This is especially the case in some of the hidden corners of Kentucky that you're going to be visiting. So take a good map, and make sure you've filled up the tank in case you make a few wrong turns along the way. And don't be afraid to stop and ask for directions. One of our favorite things about this amazing state is its people, and Kentuckians are always willing to help out a fellow Kentuckian. It's a safe bet that they'll even have at least one incredible story to tell if you take the time to ask.

A lot of patience and a good sense of humor. Even the best-laid plans go awry, and we've just told you that you aren't even required to make an official plan. So before you leave, make sure you've packed your most laid-back attitude. Things are going to go wrong; something is going to end up different than you expected it to. We promise, these unplanned treasures have been the absolute best parts of each and every one of our road trips so far. They make for the best stories; they leave you laughing the loudest. They become the stories we tell over and over. The only thing that's required of an Old Kentucky road tripper is to experience the Bluegrass State. There are going to be places that you love and places that you don't. There are going to be grand adventures, and there are going to be trips where you pull up to the gate of a state park as the park ranger locks it for the night. Accept it, laugh about it, and get back in the car. There's something else to see right around the corner.

We began this grand adventure a few years ago. As two friends who've known each other for a decade and a half and who have lived in Kentucky for all of our lives, we realized one night that there were so many parts of the state that we'd never seen. How was that even possible? We know our Kentucky geography; we got As in state history. We brag about the Derby and bourbon, about Lincoln, Sanders, Ali, Clooney, and Depp. We're Kentuckians, for crying out loud, and proud of it. But we had no idea that there was a place in the southern part of the state where an entire community gathers for a game of marbles every evening. We'd never heard of the town that boasts a dog as its mayor. We'd never had a bite of the World's Largest Country Ham and Biscuit or driven through a buffalo preserve or tasted a pawpaw fruit or set foot on a piece of the state that was entirely detached from the rest of Kentucky. Did we really know anything about Kentucky at all?

So here we are, and we invite you to join us on our quirky adventure as we set out across our home state to uncover and rediscover all of the unique and amazing things that make the Commonwealth so great. We don't do it all at once. Sometimes, months go by between our road trips. But we're always on the road, always exploring, and we know that we haven't even scratched the surface of everything there is to do and see here. So from the parkways to the back roads, here are two Kentucky natives exploring the incredibly fascinating Bluegrass State.

Keep up with the adventure with personal stories from our trips and more photos at www.myoldkentuckyroadtrip.com.

Part I

WESTERN KENTUCKY AND THE JACKSON PURCHASE

Though obtained by the United States government in 1818 from the Chickasaw Indian tribe, the eight Kentucky counties that comprise the Jackson Purchase have been considered a part of Kentucky since its statehood was ratified in 1792. If you want to be technical about it, Andrew Jackson also purchased what is now known as "West Tennessee" in the transaction, but the true Purchase region is only found in Kentucky.

Our Jackson Purchase includes landmarks like the Kentucky Bend, which separated itself from the rest of Kentucky when the Mississippi River flowed backward; Fulton County, home of the annual Fancy Farm Picnic at which Kentucky citizens become the arbiters of politicians trying to make a name for themselves; and the Land Between the Lakes, where buffalo roam and boaters can make the most of a sunny day on the water.

Go west, friends! For food and an extra hour of fun (after you cross into the Central Time Zone).

A ROAD TRIP TO THE KENTUCKY BEND

To get to the most western point of Kentucky, located in Fulton County, you have to really want to go there. Like really, really bad. The Kentucky Bend—also called the New Madrid Bend, Bessie Bend or Bubbleland (locals call it this for its teardrop shape)—is an exclave of the state. This means that it is a piece of land belonging to Kentucky that is separated from the rest of the state entirely. Surrounded by Tennessee to the south, Missouri across the Mississippi River on its other three sides, and without touching any other part of Kentucky, Bubbleland is only accessible by Tennessee State Route 22. The seventeen residents of this far-southwestern peninsula claim Tiptonville, Tennessee, as their mailing address because the town eight miles south is the nearest post office, so the kids living in the bend travel to Tiptonville each day for school. When it comes time to vote, residents make the forty-mile trip south into Tennessee and then north back into Kentucky to Hickman.

Motorists don't simply stumble onto these fifteen thousand acres. Well, it's possible to if you're really lost or if you make a wrong turn leaving Tennessee's Northwest Correctional Complex or if you're an escaped inmate. But other than that, if you're going to Bubbleland, you're going there on purpose. And you're going to have two thoughts when you arrive: "This looks like a big cornfield," and "How in the world did I get here?"

Now, the Kentucky Bend wasn't always an (almost) island unto itself. In 1812, this area of the Mississippi River was disrupted quite a bit by a series of earthquakes that occurred along the New Madrid fault line in 1811 and 1812. The way locals tell it, Bubbleland was created "when the

A sign welcomes motorists to the Kentucky Bend, or Bubbleland, the part of the state that is cut off from the rest of Kentucky by the Mississippi River.

Mighty Mississippi flowed backward" and rerouted, cutting off this bit of land from the area that would become the Jackson Purchase in 1818. The bend was claimed as part of Obion County, Tennessee, for a while, but around 1848, Kentucky's southern counterpart dropped its claim on the 17.56 square miles of mostly cropland, and it became part of the Bluegrass State. Original residents grew wheat and corn, which gave way to cotton fields in the early twentieth century. Today, the bend is primarily cornfields with a single graveyard, a few small fishing ponds, and a pretty interesting rumored history.

According to the librarian at the Hickman Public Library, the most notorious feud in Kentucky's history wasn't those pesky Hatfields and

McCoys in the far eastern part of the state. Instead, it was the violent discord that raged between the Darnell and Watson families through the late 1800s. Mark Twain made this feud famous in his memoir *Life on the Mississippi*, which was published in 1883.

"In no part of the South has the vendetta flourished more briskly, or held out longer, between warring families, than in this particular region," Twain wrote. "Every year or so, somebody was shot, on one side or the other, and as fast as one generation was laid out, their sons took up the feud and kept it a-going…And it's just as I say; they went on shooting each other, year in and year out—making a kind of religion of it, you see—till they'd done forgot, long ago, what it was all about."

The feud ended when an elderly Darnell father and his two sons decided to flee the bend by steamboat. The Watsons caught wind of this escape plan and opened fire from the riverbank, killing the younger Darnells and dousing the family line.

Now, the Kentucky Bend doesn't seem like the most likely tourist destination or Kentucky road trip stop. It's a more than six-hour trek to get there, you actually have to leave the state along your journey, and once you arrive, there's not all that much to see (and much of it is privately owned, so be friendly and polite with the locals). But you really have to make the trip.

If you go: Be prepared to get lost, and take some time to meet the locals. They can tell you (mostly true) stories about the history of this region that you won't find in the history books, and they can help you get just about anywhere. They can also be counted on to help travelers change a tire when you pick up a nail on one of those backcountry roads.

What it costs: Not a thing, except a tank or two of gas and a stop for lunch along the way. Skip fast food and look for one of the unique local diners. If you pass through Madisonville, Hopkinsville, or Cadiz on your journey, grab a cheeseburger at Ferrell's Hamburgers. This family-owned mini-chain of three restaurants cooks up some of the best burgers in the state. President Bill Clinton once enjoyed a lunch at the Hopkinsville location.

How to get there: Take Purchase Parkway to U.S. 51 to Kentucky 94, which leads through Hickman and south into Tennessee. From there, connect with Tennessee 78 and then through a round of detours—all surprisingly well marked along a very rural, two-lane route—to Tennessee 22 heading north. You'll pass a few graveyards that dot the thousands of acres of corn, soybeans, and sweet sorghum that fill this region; a state jail; and some friendly locals. And to get back out of Bubbleland, there's no other way but to retrace your steps.

If you spend the weekend: Take some time back across the Mississippi River to explore Hickman, Kentucky. The locals boast that Mark Twain once called Hickman the "Most Beautiful Town on the Mississippi," and it certainly has a picturesque appeal. Take the ferry across the river to Dorena, Missouri, and back. The captains are a blast to talk to, and for just two dollars each way, they'll take passengers on foot to get a river view of the Kentucky banks and chat with you the entire ride (except for the docking and undocking part, which is important). And if you make your trip in September, try to go the weekend that Hickman hosts the Pecan Festival.

The riverboat ferry crosses the Mississippi River from Hickman, Kentucky, to Dorena, Missouri. You can travel on foot for two dollars each way if you want the opportunity to see Kentucky from the Mississippi River.

2

A ROAD TRIP TO LAND BETWEEN THE LAKES

They call it "God's Country." The minute you pull off of the Pennyrile Parkway into Trigg and Christian Counties, you'll hear it from the lips of everyone you pass. In God's Country, the weather is always perfect; it never rains. Here, people are good to their neighbors; they take care of one another. It's the perfect place to raise a family; it's the most beautiful place in Kentucky. Now, while not all of these things are completely accurate (it does rain there on fairly regular occasion, as is needed to nurture the region's bountiful cropland), there is something to be said about a place whose residents take such a strong pride in preserving, protecting, and promoting. And while officially changing the region's motto to "God's Country" would be open for much debate, there is no denying that the Land Between the Lakes in western Kentucky is one of the state's most incredible hidden treasures.

Tucked in between Kentucky Lake—often called Ken Lake in these parts—and Lake Barkley, Land Between the Lakes is a National Recreation Area managed by the United States Department of Agriculture Forest Service. It is a natural sanctuary with beautiful views and a lot to see and do. Founded in 1963, this family-friendly recreation area is one of the largest blocks of undeveloped forest in the eastern United States. More than 170,000 acres of forests, wetlands, and open lands lie on a peninsula between these two lakes, including three hundred miles of natural shoreline and ideal opportunities for camping, picnicking, hiking, fishing, boating, water sports, and the chance to spot some pretty unique wildlife.

Lighthouse Landing Marina overlooks Lake Barkley from Land Between the Lakes National Recreation Area. It is one of many lodging opportunities in the area.

In just one weekend, snag a largemouth bass or paddlefish, spot a bald eagle, and drive among elk and bison in their native grassland habitat. You also have the chance to take a look back in time at this region of Kentucky in the 1850s. The Homeplace, a working farm that is open March through November, represents a two-generation farm in the late nineteenth century. Interpreters in period clothing go about their daily chores while visitors explore artifacts and restored historic structures and hear stories of the history of western Kentucky before the Civil War.

You've never seen hard work like this. Forget the chainsaws and table saws—these workers split rails for fence boards with heavy axes. But don't get lured in by the tempting smells of hardy country cooking coming from the wood-burning stove. If you get too close, the ladies will likely be inclined to ask you to help.

When you finish churning your butter, take a short trip into the woods between Honker and Hematite Lakes, where you'll find the Nature Station staffed by wildlife specialists who can help you spot even the most elusive creatures. Spot great horned owls, coyotes, and red wolves, and if you time it just right, you can take part in an educational program about wildlife, gardening, and nature photography.

Fishermen on Kentucky Lake near the dam. Kentucky Lake is the western boundary of Land Between the Lakes National Recreation Area.

Still not enough? As if the stars don't shine bright enough over the sparkling waters formed by the Cumberland and Tennessee Rivers that created Land Between the Lakes, you can also pick out the constellations during the day at the Golden Pond Planetarium and Observatory.

If you go: You'll need a bathing suit (if the weather is warm enough), some comfortable hiking shoes, and your binoculars. Take some time to experience all of the unique things these 170,000 acres have to offer, and don't hesitate to try something new: jump on that jet ski or bait your own hook—it can be a weekend of firsts for you. This region gets hot in the summer and boasts amazing views in the spring and fall months. The cool winter months are the best time to spot a bald eagle.

What it costs: Well, that all depends on how much you want to see and do. If you want to simply drive down the forty-mile peninsula, that's between you and your gas tank. But if you take part in some of the exceptional attractions, there are a few small fees (nothing over seven dollars within the recreation area). You can find the most up-to-date costs at www.landbetweenthelakes.us.

How to get there: The easiest way to access Land Between the Lakes is via U.S. 68 coming from Trigg County on the Lake Barkley side or Murray, Kentucky, on the Kentucky Lake side. You can also enter from I-24 via Kentucky 253, also known as the "Trace" or "Woodlands Trace," which travels through Grand Rivers and then the entire length of the peninsula.

If you spend the weekend: Take the weekend and book a night at one of the spectacular state parks in the area or at one of the beautiful lodging opportunities along the lakes. Lake Barkley State Resort Park and Kentucky Lake State Park boast beautiful lodges, private cottages, and cabins and some of the best food around. Take U.S. 68 to the western side of Ken Lake and stop at Belew's Dairy Bar for a burger and milkshake before spending an evening at one of the great miniature golf courses on the same road.

 ELK AND BISON PRAIRIE

If you want to experience a home where the buffalo roam, head to the untouched natural sanctuary of Land Between the Lakes in western Kentucky. The Elk and Bison Prairie offers a native grassland habitat that was common in this region of the state more than a century ago. Today, elk and bison roam free within this seven-hundred-acre enclosure, offering visitors a rare opportunity for a close-up but safe view of these native species.

The Elk and Bison Prairie in Land Between the Lakes National Recreation Area is protected by the United States Department of Agriculture and allows visitors a safe way to get close to these animals.

You'll enter through a gate, pay a small fee, and remain in your enclosed vehicle nearly the entire time. This is for the safety of both you and the animals, and it absolutely will not keep you from getting up close and personal with a few bison. While the elk tend to be a bit more skittish and are easier to spot in the distance, the bison can often be found lying right on the edge of the road and will walk beside your car as you drive through. Be careful, they've been known to nudge a few cars. Don't get discouraged if you don't spot any right away, as the three-and-a-half-mile paved loop through the prairie offers plenty of time to view these animals and others, including wild turkeys, a variety of birds, and small game.

In the spring, visitors can see the elk and bison shedding their winter coats. In May, the first bison calves appear. Elk calves come later in May or in June. Elk keep their newborn calves hidden in vegetation until they are strong enough to keep up with the herd. Also during the spring months, the forest service begins controlled burns to remove dead grasses and deter tree growth on the prairie. In the summer, elk and bison seek relief from the hot days under shade trees or in the pond. In early fall, the prairie wildflowers are in bloom, and the elk begin bugling, which is their mating call. The animals rub the bark off trees, polishing their antlers around this time of year. Because of the bare landscape, the winter months are the best times for seeing wildlife. The elk and bison have their full winter coats by December and can be found grazing in the grass fields throughout the day when it is cold. Whenever you're visiting, keep in mind that the animals are most active just after sunrise and just before sunset.

In addition to the Elk and Bison Prairie, visitors can find bison roaming in two adjacent one-hundred-acre pastures at the South Bison Range, located along the Woodlands Trace across from the Homeplace, south of the Tennessee state line. Be careful during mating season (July to September), as bulls are especially aggressive and have been known to charge.

Kentucky's Famous Food Festivals

Cured country hams hang in a tent near the courthouse on Main Street waiting to find out if they are grand-prize winners. Kids are fighting nausea on their third turn on the Tilt-A-Whirl in the nearby park; arts and crafts booths line the streets along with food vendors offering deep-fried Snickers, Twinkies, pickles, and everything else your stomach can dream up. And in the center of it all, the World's Largest Country Ham and Biscuit bakes in its custom-made oven-trailer.

Kentucky food festivals are things of pride, and locals travel to their favorite feasts year after year to take part in these one-of-a-kind celebrations of food culture and undeniably unique traditions. Cadiz, Kentucky, has celebrated country ham with the four-day Trigg County Country Ham Festival on each second weekend of October since 1977. Its Guiness World Record–official huge biscuit debuted in 1985 during the ninth-annual ham festival. It weighed four thousand pounds, and a crowd of more than fifteen thousand people were on hand to view the biscuit and parade in its honor, grand marshaled by University of Kentucky basketball coach Joe B. Hall.

The Trigg County Country Ham Festival, which takes place on the second weekend of October each year, is home to the Guiness World Record–holding World's Largest Country Ham and Biscuit.

Still prepared each year for the festival, the recipe has since been halved, and each year a 2,000-pound version, measuring ten and a half feet in diameter, is baked in a custom-built oven and removed by forklift during the festival. The recipe includes 150 pounds of flour, 2 pounds of salt, 6.5 pounds of sugar, 39 pounds of shortening, 39 cups of water, and 13 gallons of buttermilk. Add 16 large country hams, and it is served to the masses. What a reason to celebrate!

If the salty country ham isn't your thing (it is an acquired taste), head to one of the many other food festivals sprinkled across the state each year. Don't miss a single taste of Kentucky.

Tater Days in Benton: This has been a tradition since 1842, when local sweet potato seedlings were distributed to boost local agriculture. Today, the festive trade day is celebrated on the first Monday in April and is regarded as the oldest continuously celebrated day of its kind in the country.

Barbecue Festival in Danville: Some of the best smokers in the state come out for this weekend event, and locals stand in lines that extend multiple blocks for a taste of what they're cooking.

Beer Cheese Festival in Winchester: The second Saturday of each June, this community gets together to eat beer cheese and determine the best recipes in various categories.

Pecan Festival in Hickman: In September, folks in this Mississippi River town gather for a community-wide yard sale, arts and crafts, and to celebrate this delicious tree nut.

Burgoo Festival in Lawrenceburg: Not many people outside of Kentucky know what burgoo is. This spicy stew of veggies and whatever meat you have laying around is honored and devoured in Anderson County each September.

Kentucky Bourbon Festival in Bardstown: Not a food? Think again. In Kentucky, bourbon is the most important food group there is. Since 1776, the people of Bardstown have been making bourbon. Their dedication to this fine art made the town the Bourbon Capital of the World, and locals laud this passion and history for six days of smooth bourbon, delicious food, and Kentucky hospitality each year.

Funny Place Names

Oh, Kentucky…we love you and your matchless brand of individualism and town pride. Here we present, in no particular order, our favorite funny, unique, weird, and wonderful Kentucky place names.

Possum Trot is an actual town. It's a dot on the map in Marshall County, Kentucky, east of Paducah. On the western side of that western Kentucky town, you'll find **Monkeys Eyebrow**—note, that is not a possessive "monkey's"—in Ballard County (your GPS will pretend the place doesn't exist, despite the signs that say it is so). Officially, it isn't actually a town because it has never had a post office, but don't say that to the locals.

Rabbit Hash is really just a general store and a couple shops along the river in Boone County on Kentucky 536, just southwest of Cincinnati. Supposedly, the name comes from the recipe that helped the town residents survive a harsh flood in 1816. Their mayor is a dog for which the residents vote at a cost of one dollar per vote to raise money for improvements to the town.

Mud Lick. There are actually ten towns with this name in Kentucky. You'll find them in Anderson, Elliott, Greenup, Knox, Lewis, Monroe, Perry, Pike, Robertson, and Russell Counties. This isn't to be confused with **Paint Lick** in Garrard County.

88—yes, you read that right—is in Barren County on Kentucky 90, a few miles south of Glasgow. It is rumored to get its name from the fact that one of the town's founders had eighty-eight cents in his pocket when they were trying to pick a name. Talk about running out of ideas. Other rumors say the local postmaster had such terrible handwriting that he picked the name because he was sure everyone could read those two numerals.

Future City in Ballard County. This town reportedly got its name from the developer who put up a sign at the edge of the land where he intended to build a town that read "Future City." And then he never got around to building anything.

There are two towns named **Lamb**, one in Kenton County and the other in Monroe County.

Bush in Laurel County was named after George Bush. No, not *that* George Bush. No, not that one either. This George Bush founded the town in 1840 when he opened the post office and general store. The first President Bush did campaign there in 1988, and newspaper headlines read "Bush Returns to Bush."

Bugtussle on Kentucky 87 south of Tompkinsville in Monroe County is popular with fans of *The Beverly Hillbillies*, who may remember that the Clampetts were from Bugtussle...only they were from Bugtussle, Tennessee. Monroe County *is* near the Tennessee border.

Other creatively named dots on the map (or not on the map) include:

Black Gnat in Taylor County.
Black Snake in Bell County.
Co-operative in McCreary County.
Crummies in Harlan County.
Hi Hat (as in "hello") in Floyd County.
Quality in Butler County.
Subtle in Metcalfe County.
Susie in Wayne County.
Whoopee Hill in Ohio County.
Wild Cat in Clay County.

3
A ROAD TRIP TO FANCY FARM

Your average church picnic might conjure up images of potluck suppers, neighbors sharing a picnic table, or children playing across the lawn. When you attend St. Jerome Catholic Church's Annual Picnic in Fancy Farm, Kentucky, fellowship and meals shared among friends becomes a loud, raucous political rally where the color red or blue obligates you to cheer (or jeer) the candidates delivering their stump speeches underneath the Lyin' Tree.

Ongoing as a church and charity fundraiser since 1880, St. Jerome's Annual Picnic, known simply as "Fancy Farm" across the Commonwealth, captures the full attention of the nation during contentious election years. Upward of fifteen thousand people attend annually and consume more than eighteen thousand pounds of barbecue mutton and pork while listening to candidates speak from the platform. The largest recorded attendance was in 1992, when nearly twenty thousand people turned out to see Bill Clinton and Al Gore.

Fancy Farm, Kentucky, itself counted its population at only 458 in the last census, and it takes all those citizens and more to pull off the largest political event in the state. More than 600 volunteers work tirelessly each year to smoke pork and mutton, fry chicken, set up and clean up what can only reasonably be described as a hootenanny.

Every candidate gets an equal voice at Fancy Farm. The two major political parties line up their candidates, testimonials from prominent party members, and their loudest volunteers and supporters to make a showing at the rally.

Though the parties are very clearly split—Democrats to one side of the podium, Republicans to the other—the crowd is actually very genial,

Fancy Farm Picnic is a statewide political gathering and church picnic that happens each year in August.

if not downright friendly. We never saw a single person heckled for a particular lobby they were espousing or candidate they were supporting, though trust us, the candidates were heckled plenty. Colorfully dressed characters from both sides roam through the crowds with their particular shtick. In particular, a fellow dressed as Uncle Sam seemed to be everywhere with plenty of signage, buttons, and a loud voice with which to spread his opinions.

We spent most of our day wandering through the crowd, scoping out the various carnival games, entering the raffle to win a car—a tradition since 1924—and, of course, eating barbecue. You have to try the barbecue nachos, a recent addition to the menu.

St. Jerome Catholic Church held the first-annual church picnic in 1880 "down by the creek," according to local oral histories. The event was moved to a location near the local elementary school in the 1910s to offer shelter in case of bad weather.

The picnic has always been held on a late summer weekend, or in other terms, close to Election Day. Such a large gathering of citizens was an opportunity for local and state candidates to come and make their final pleas to voters underneath the old oak tree in front of the school. The so-called

Lyin' Tree was struck by lightning in 1974, but the stump remains behind with a plaque that reads:

> *Lightning struck this 133-year-old oak tree on April 15, 1974. The tree trunk remains a symbol of the years since 1880 where political speeches were made on the first Saturday in August at the Fancy Farm annual picnic. Some of America's greatest statesmen have spoken under the shade of this great oak tree.*

Former Republican governor Louie Nunn joked at the 1979 picnic that the tree had died as a result of all the political speeches over the years, saying, "Too much fertilizer will kill anything."

Nunn has a place on a long and illustrious list of politicians who have campaigned at Fancy Farm, including Vice President Alben Barkley, Senator John Sherman Cooper, and Governors AB "Happy" Chandler, Wendell Ford, John Y. Brown, and Martha Layne Collins. The picnic was a flashpoint for the 2014 United States Senate race between challenger Allison Lundergan Grimes and victorious incumbent Mitch McConnell.

State and national political candidates have gathered to debate—or give stump speeches—at Fancy Farm each year since 1880.

Being sponsored by the St. Jerome Parish, the political events of the day start with prayer and the state song and national anthem. As every native Kentuckian knows, it's hard not to swell with pride while singing the state song surrounded by thousands of friends from the Bluegrass State. Then the candidates come out.

Surrounded by staffers, supporters, family, and the state police, the crowd propels the speaker onto the dais (newly renovated to look like a front porch with fans to keep the speakers cool) amidst yelling supporters and critics. From there it's lights, camera, action, with scores of local and national media reporting the scene for those who didn't attend.

Never is the term "stump speech" more clearly defined than at Fancy Farm. Candidates are (almost literally) delivering their campaign promises from a stump. The proceedings are much too large and engineered now for anyone to actually stand atop a tree stump, but you get the gist.

And it's not like there's really anything new to say at Fancy Farm. Most folks are there as supporters of a particular candidate, and it's hard to imagine the majority go with an open mind that could be swayed. In fact, Fancy Farm has become a sort of pan-generational tradition where the good old boys pass on their connections and handshakes to the up-and-coming movers and shakers of the various political parties.

That being said, Fancy Farm is an Experience—capital E. For a state with such a diverse political climate, the small, deeply rooted Kentucky town is the quintessential locale for such a unique tradition. Travelers with an open mind shouldn't miss a yearly opportunity to convene with colorful characters and bombastic politicians or to treat themselves to a good meal that's been more than 130 years in the making.

If you go: It will be HOT! We're talking the first weekend in August in a Southern town, in a large field without much shade. Dress comfortably, wear good walking shoes that you don't mind getting a bit dirty, and don't forget sunscreen.

What it costs: Nothing. Unless you want to eat barbecue, and you do want to eat barbecue. Plan to bring cash with some decent variation amongst your bills; you don't want to be the rude person in the concessions line holding fifteen thousand people up because you were waiting on change.

How to get there: It's incredibly easy to make the drive down to Graves County. Take the Western Kentucky Parkway and the Purchase Parkway toward Mayfield, then up Kentucky 80 to Fancy Farm. You can also navigate by the density of political signs along the road as you drive, but that's less precise.

If you spend the weekend: Your best bet is to backtrack toward the state resort parks at the Land Between the Lakes, or book a hotel room in nearby Paducah. But book ahead of time! Western Kentucky hotels fill up quickly for this weekend.

NATIONAL QUILT MUSEUM

The art of quilting is far older than the state of Kentucky—it dates back to years that end in BC—but it is woven into the history and culture of the state and remains an important tradition today. This is particularly true in historic downtown Paducah, where you can visit the National Quilt Museum, one of the most respected and well-known organizations among quilting enthusiasts.

Since it opened more than two decades ago, the National Quilt Museum has aimed to support quilters and advance the art of quilting by displaying exceptional quilt and fiber art exhibits, providing workshops and educational opportunities, and promoting the unique art of quilting. Over the years, the museum has grown, and today it is a destination for quilting and fiber art enthusiasts from around the world. Visitors from all fifty states and more than forty foreign countries arrive each year to view the museum's diverse on-site and traveling exhibits.

The museum was founded by quilting enthusiasts and Paducah residents Bill and Meredith Schroeder. They wanted to open a place to celebrate the work of today's quilters and establish an environment to bring the art form to new audiences. This one-of-a-kind attraction rotates its exhibits eight to ten times per year, so each visit is fresh and unique. The museum also continually strives to expand its collection, which began with just 85 quilts on loan. Today, the museum is home to

The National Quilt Museum in Paducah is a nationally recognized art museum that exhibits the finest quilting and fiber art in the world. *Photo via iStock.*

more than 320 works of art and hosts regular traveling exhibits of quilt and fiber art throughout the year. For a schedule of upcoming exhibits, visit the National Quilt Museum website at www.quiltmuseum.org.

Visit these sources for additional information on the destinations and topics covered:
- *Fulton County, Kentucky: www.fultoncounty.ky.gov*
- *City of Hickman: www.hickman.cityof.org*
- *United States Department of Agriculture Forest Service: www.landbetweenthelakes.us/about/overview*
- *United States Department of Agriculture Forest Service—Land Between the Lakes—Elk and Bison Prairie: www.landbetweenthelakes.us/seendo/attractions/elk-bison-prairie*
- *Fancy Farm Picnic: www.fancyfarm.net/uploads/The_Annual_Picnic_at_Fancy_Farm.pdf*
- *National Quilt Museum: www.quiltmuseum.org*

──────── *Part II* ────────

THE PENNYRILE

Pennyroyal, or *Hedeoma pulegioides*, is a small, pale blue plant native to western Kentucky. It's also where the Pennyrile region gets its name. Once home to both Abraham Lincoln *and* Jefferson Davis, the Pennyrile is the largest Kentucky region. We've included both the Knobs—an area of small, round hills between the Bluegrass Region and western Kentucky—and the Western Coal Field in our definition of the Pennyrile.

Perhaps the biggest geographical feature of the Pennyrile, and we mean "biggest" literally, is Mammoth Cave National Park. The longest cave system in the world, Mammoth Cave is twice as long as the second-longest cave, Sac Actun in Mexico.

What are other can't-miss opportunities in the Pennyrile? Fort Knox, to live out your James Bond fantasies, and the Wigwam Village, truly the most unique hotel accommodations in the state.

4
A ROAD TRIP TO THE JEFFERSON DAVIS MONUMENT

When you're driving down U.S. 68 between Hopkinsville and Russellville, you're going to come upon a tall—351 feet, to be exact—obelisk towering over the trees. This shrine looks an awful lot like the Washington Monument was pulled out of the ground in D.C. and planted right in the middle of Fairview, Kentucky. But this structure is a tribute to Jefferson Davis, the first and only president of the Confederacy, who was born in Fairview in 1807.

Davis was president of the Confederate States of America during the Civil War from 1861 to 1865. He was born in Kentucky to a farmer and moved to Mississippi and then Louisiana to work on his brother's cotton plantations before attending West Point. He fought in the Mexican-American War (1846–48), served as the United States secretary of war from 1853 to 1857, and was a United States senator from Mississippi.

Now, there is a bit of controversy when discussing a memorial to the president of the Confederate States, but politics and sordid history aside, this accomplished general is from Kentucky, and Kentuckians don't shy away from honoring their own. So the Bluegrass State stands alone in its ability to have a memorial to the sixteenth president of the United States, Abraham Lincoln, who was born at Sinking Spring Farm and led the country through the Civil War, and a memorial to Jefferson Davis, the president of the Confederate States.

This monument stands in Fairview in honor of the first and only president of the Confederacy, Jefferson Davis, who is a Kentucky native.

The view from the top of the 351-foot obelisk Jefferson Davis Monument in Fairview.

Simon Bolivar Buckner Sr. was the Confederate general who first proposed the idea for a monument honoring Davis. The Daughters of the Confederacy and the Orphan Brigade of the Confederate army funded the project with $200,000. It began construction in 1917 but stopped a year later at only 175 feet due to building material rationing during World War I. Construction ultimately resumed in 1922 and was finished two years later. The structure is made of more than 300,000 tons of unreinforced concrete and extends 19 feet under the ground where it is anchored on a bed of limestone. It is the third-tallest obelisk in the world, behind the San Jacinto Monument in Texas and the Washington Monument in Washington, D.C.

An observatory is located at the top of the monument that looks out over the Pennyrile region. Pilot Rock—a popular rock climbing attraction in nearby Elkton—can be seen in the distance from one of the windows. Originally, this room was only accessible by stairs, but an elevator was installed in 1929—so don't worry, everyone has the opportunity to see Kentucky from the top.

MY OLD KENTUCKY ROAD TRIP

If you go: In addition to walking around the beautifully manicured grounds and visiting the gift shop, make the trip up the elevator to the observation level. The views from the top are incredible and the tour guide has lots of great information about the monument and about Jefferson Davis's history in the Commonwealth.

What it costs: There's no charge just to walk around the grounds and poke around the gift shop, but to enter the museum in the visitor center and to ride the elevator to the top requires a small fee. For the most up-to-date pricing information, visit parks.ky.gov/parks/historicsites/jefferson-davis.

How to get there: Hop on U.S. 68, which spans the length of the state, and get off at Jefferson Davis Road in Fairview just before Kentucky 115. Signs make this easy to find (not to mention the obelisk on the horizon).

If you spend the weekend: The Pennyrile is a region full of interesting places to visit and things to see. While traveling down U.S. 68, you'll go right through Hopkinsville, Russellville, and into Bowling Green. If you're in the far west, visit Land Between the Lakes in Trigg County. In Bowling Green, visit the National Corvette Museum.

5
A ROAD TRIP TO LINCOLN'S BIRTHPLACE

Kentucky is a pretty cool place that asserts bragging rights to a lot of unique and interesting claims to fame. Perhaps one of its proudest and most debated attributes is being the birthplace of Abraham Lincoln, the sixteenth president of the United States.

Illinois calls itself the "Land of Lincoln," and the state where Lincoln moved to work as an adult takes a lot of credit for Honest Abe's ideals and philosophies. All apologies to Kentucky's neighbors to the north, but you can only be born in one place, and Kentucky is proud to take credit for providing some of the foundational beliefs that the future president absorbed during his childhood.

Lincoln was born on a farm in LaRue County, Kentucky. His parents, Thomas and Nancy Lincoln, and sister moved from nearby Elizabethtown to Sinking Spring Farm a few months before baby Abraham was born. His father paid two hundred dollars for 348 acres of stony ground on the south fork of Nolin Creek called Sinking Spring Farm, named for a spring on the property that emerged from a deep cave and dropped water into a bottomless pit. Thomas Lincoln moved to Kentucky as a boy in 1782, just seven years after Daniel Boone pioneered the uncharted region that then belonged to Virginia. He was a farmer and a carpenter who married Nancy Hanks in 1806. Two years later, Thomas purchased the Sinking Spring acreage. Just two years after Abraham was born, Thomas Lincoln lost this land in a title dispute and moved his family down the road to the Knob Creek Farm, where the family would live from 1811 until 1816. As you're driving through

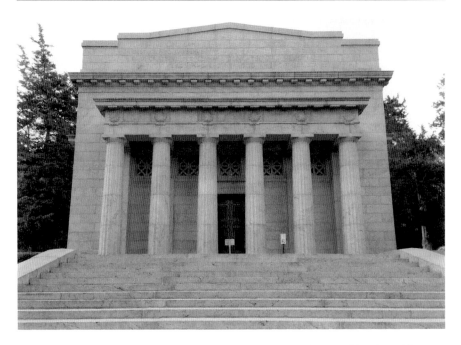

A monument to the sixteenth president of the United States, Abraham Lincoln, at his birthplace at Sinking Spring Farm near Hodgenville.

Hodgenville following signs to the president's birthplace, you'll actually pass the Knob Creek boyhood home.

As the country's first memorial to Lincoln, the Sinking Spring Farm has welcomed visitors for more than a century. At this National Historic Site, you can still walk down to the farm's namesake, Sinking Spring, where the Lincoln family got its water. Then, head up to the visitor's center where you'll find information and exhibits, including artifacts like the Lincoln family Bible with the signatures of Abraham's father and mother. You'll also be invited to study the Lincoln family tree and to watch a brief orientation film about Lincoln's early life in Kentucky. And for the Lincoln super fans, go ahead and pick up your Honest Abe Top Hat before you make the climb up to his cabin and memorial.

There are a lot of rumors circulating about the authenticity of the cabin that now stands inside the memorial building at Sinking Spring. It is often joked that Lincoln was born in three states (because of the claims staked by Kentucky, Indiana, and Illinois) and in at least two cabins (the original and the reconstructed). Historians today acknowledge that the cabin that stands in the memorial in Hodgenville includes only part of the original logs of

Above: President Abraham Lincoln was born in a small, one-room cabin on Sinking Spring Farm near what is now Hodgenville. Today, his birthplace is safely kept inside a monument built to honor the country's sixteenth president.

Right: This spring is the namesake of Sinking Spring Farm, the land President Abraham Lincoln's father, Thomas Lincoln, owned in Kentucky when baby Abraham was born. The Lincolns lost the land two years later in a dispute over the ownership of the acreage.

the Lincoln family cabin where Abraham was born. The original log cabin was dismantled sometime before 1865. A New York businessman purchased the Lincoln farm in 1894 and assembled an exhibition to take on the road. He used the logs from the original cabin as well as logs from a nearby house to construct a cabin similar in appearance to the one where Lincoln was born. Then, he moved it from city to city around the country dismantling and re-erecting his display. By the time the Lincoln Farm Association purchased the Lincoln logs from the businessman, some of the original logs had been mixed up with other cabin logs. As rumor has it, some of the logs belonged to the cabin at the present-day Jefferson Davis memorial site in western Kentucky. Today, the cabin that is erected inside the memorial building stands twelve feet by seventeen feet, the approximate size of the original cabin, allowing visitors to look into the tiny home where the sixteenth president of the United States came into this world. Whether or not all of those logs are original to Sinking Spring is still up for debate, but it doesn't deter visitors from honoring their hometown president at the historic site.

The memorial building was designed by John Russell Pope and features sixteen windows, sixteen rosettes on the ceiling, and sixteen fence poles. Seeing a pattern here? The fifty-six steps leading up to the building entrance represent his age at his death. The cornerstone of the memorial building was laid by President Theodore Roosevelt in 1909, and two years later, the building was dedicated by President William Howard Taft. The construction was paid for with donations.

If you go: Pack bug spray, and be mindful of the park hours. Check the National Park Service website before you go for the most up-to-date times. You don't want your experience cut short because the park is closing on you. Make sure you have plenty of time to walk through the museum, climb up to the memorial building, and make your way down to the infamous Sinking Spring. Be sure to read through some of the guest book entries in the visitor center to see just from how far and wide guests have traveled, and add your name to the list.

What it cost you: Admission is free to walk around the National Historic Site. Donations are welcomed inside the gift shop.

How to get there: Easily accessible from I-65 or from the Bluegrass Parkway to U.S. 31 East through Hodgenville. Signs every few miles will lead you straight there.

If you stay the weekend: Stay in and explore nearby Hodgenville and the Knob Creek Farm. As close as you'll be to it (likely passing it on your way to Sinking Spring on U.S. 31 East), you don't want to miss this important part of the president's childhood. You'll be an easy drive away from the breathtaking Abbey of Gethsemani, where you absolutely have to watch the sunset.

6

A ROAD TRIP TO THE ABBEY OF GETHSEMANI

Road trips are often filled with laughter and conversation and a really great playlist. In some very rare cases, road trips are completely silent. And it's not because your travel companion messed up the directions and has you miles off track or because your MP3 player's battery is dead. When you travel to the Abbey of Gethsemani near Bardstown, your trip will be silent because that is part of the experience: quiet reflection.

Monks in white robes and black scapulars move about the grounds crossing themselves and keeping their heads bowed in contemplation and reflection. Hands clasped and eyes looking up, they stand in a long, unbroken silence.

For many who aren't familiar with the Catholic faith or the practices of monasteries and abbeys, this destination will be very different from some of the other trips you'll take across the state. Here, Trappist monks who have taken vows of obedience, stability, and conversion of manners live, pray, and work together. The monks are a part of the Order of Cistercians of the Strict Observance, and they follow the Rule of Saint Benedict by living a contemplative life of faithful prayer and work.

Gethsemani was founded in 1848 and is the oldest monastery in the United States that is still in operation. It is built on a two-thousand-acre working farm that allows the monks to support themselves by making handmade Trappist cheeses, fruitcake, and fudge.

Admission into the abbey's ranks is a long and difficult process. Before being admitted, an individual must pass a series of psychological tests, and

A statue overlooks the Abbey of Gethsemani on a full moon.

The Abbey of Gethsemani is a Roman Catholic monastery where Thomas Merton once took his vows.

once accepted, he spends six months as a postulant before being given a white robe. He spends two years as a novice monk, and then, if found to be capable, he is approved and becomes a junior monk. Individuals only become fully professed monks after at least three years of preparation and taking solemn vows.

Guests are welcome and may roam around the abbey and its surrounding trails, woodlands, and fields, but get used to the sound of silence. If you're interested in staying for a retreat, Gethsemani offers a silent and unstructured opportunity. Men and women are welcome to book a retreat but will be staying during different weeks. Speaking is only allowed in designated areas, and visitors are expected to respect the rules.

Gethsemani was home to social activist, author and Trappist monk Thomas Merton from 1941 until his death in 1968. Merton wrote about issues including spirituality and social justice. His autobiography, *The Seven Storey Mountain* (1948), which details his spiritual journey, has made the Abbey of Gethsemani a popular stop for tourists and Merton fans. Merton is buried in the cemetery at the abbey, his grave marked by a uniform small white metal cross that reads "Fr. Louis Merton, Died Dec. 10, 1968." It matches all of the others.

If you go: Stepping out of your comfort zone might not sound like a relaxing vacation, but being willing to travel to somewhere that you've never been and have an experience you may not normally consider is one of the best ways to begin an adventure. Be respectful of others while you are there, and pay attention to the signs—these will designate areas you are allowed to walk in and areas where conversation is permitted.

What it costs: There is no cost to visit the abbey.

How to get there: The easiest way to get there is to take Bluegrass Parkway to U.S. 31 East toward Hodgenville. Turn on Kentucky 247, or Monks Road, and follow the signs to the abbey.

7
A ROAD TRIP TO
FORT KNOX

Whether it's James Bond saving the country's gold supply from Auric Goldfinger or an alien race tricking humans into mining the gold out of the United States' supply in *Battlefield Earth* (2000), the United States Bullion Depository at Fort Knox is one of the most curious and intriguing of all of secrets kept by the country's Treasury Department.

Often simply called Fort Knox for its location inside the United States army base, the United States Bullion Depository is a fortified vault building used to store a large portion of the country's gold reserves and other precious items entrusted to the federal government. Because there hasn't been an official audit of the depository since the 1930s, the exact contents of the vault are unknown. However, it is estimated that the depository holds roughly 3 percent of all the gold ever refined throughout human history.

The depository was built in 1936 to provide a place for the Federal Reserve to hold its gold. Because President Franklin D. Roosevelt had outlawed private ownership of gold coins, bullion, and certificates three years earlier, the government had a whole lot of gold that had been turned in by citizens and nowhere to keep it all. The gold vault was completed in December 1936. A fortress-like structure stands over an underground vault lined with granite walls and protected by a blast-proof door weighing twenty-two tons. So don't get any ideas, Danny Ocean. Beyond the twenty-one-inch-thick main vault door, smaller compartments provide further protection. The entire facility is guarded by the United States Mint Police, and the United States Army provides additional protection at its Fort Knox post. And this hasn't even touched on the security measures yet. The depository is protected by every possible physical

The entrance to Fort Knox Army Post in West Point, Kentucky. Fort Knox is home to the United States Bullion Depository, where the country stores a great deal of its gold resources.

security measure, including alarms, video cameras, minefields, barbed razor wire, electric fences, and heavily armed guards. An escape tunnel from the vault's lower level was built for any person who might be accidentally locked in.

For these extensive security reasons, no visitors have been allowed inside the depository grounds since the vault opened. Exceptions have included members of the United States Congress and the very rare news media access. But even without getting to go inside, visitors can take photos of the structure from the road, and it's pretty cool to stand so close to such a fortune.

So just how much gold is in Fort Knox? Today, approximately 4,578 metric tons, or 147.2 million troy ounces, are housed in the depository. This gold is in the form of 368,000 standard 400.0–troy ounce gold bars. At the present gold rate, that totals approximately $238.290 billion. But even with that fortune, Fort Knox comes in second behind the Federal Reserve Bank of New York's underground vault in Manhattan, which holds 7,000 metric tons of gold bullion.

The bullion depository at Fort Knox isn't the only part of the army base that is worth seeing. While you're there, make sure you tour the rest of the base, which covers a total of 109,054 acres spanning three Kentucky counties—Bullitt, Hardin, and Meade. There, the United States Army works to develop cutting-edge technology to enhance training and readiness of troops for war. There, you can also tour the General George Patton Museum.

If you go: Be mindful that Fort Knox is a fully operational army base, so be respectful of rules and regulations and where you can and cannot go, but don't hesitate to ask for help. There are a lot of very helpful professionals around the base. Special arrangements need to be made ahead of time in order to tour the base. The bullion depository is closed to all visitors unless you work for the Treasury Department or the United States Mint—or if you're a United States senator, but even that won't guarantee you access. For more information to help you plan your visit, go to www.knox.army.mil/About/Information.

What it costs: Nothing just to drive around the base.

How to get there: Fort Knox is easily accessible off I-65 at Elizabethtown. Take U.S. 31 West into Fort Knox.

If you spend the weekend: You're just a short drive from Louisville on I-65, or head back through Elizabethtown, which is a convenient central location to easily get to many Kentucky attractions. West of Elizabethtown, visit Abraham Lincoln's birthplace in Hodgenville, or head east on the Bluegrass Parkway to Bardstown and sample a few of the bourbon flavors that Kentucky is known for.

HOW THE PENNYRILE GOT ITS NAME

One of the best things about Kentucky is its rich histories, charming traditions, and tall tales. Often, lessons on the history of the state are derived from stories that have been told over and over until they are basically somewhat almost true—or at least everyone has gotten to add their versions to the narrative. One of the best tales in the western part of the state is the history of the Pennyrile region and how it got its name.

The most widely accepted version of the story, according to the director of the Pennyroyal Area Museum in Hopkinsville, is that early English settlers in the area saw an abundant little minty plant that smelled a whole lot like the pennyroyal plant found in England. So they started referring to the area as the place where pennyroyal could be found. The mispronunciation of the pennyroyal name came from Kentuckians simply saying it wrong for so many years. The southern Kentucky dialect changed the way people accented the word, and they started spelling it like they said it. So if you see Pennyrile or Pennyroyal, know it's referring to the same thing.

If you're in the Pennyrile region, you'll see an abundance of Kentucky pennyroyal. Unlike its English ground-covering counterpart, the Kentucky version is slightly taller—growing about twelve inches high—and more tree-like. It has tiny leaves and small lavender flowers that bloom for a short two-week period. It is said to have medicinal values, like helping to relieve headaches and itchy eyes.

8

A ROAD TRIP TO RABBIT HASH

In a uniquely named town in the northern part of the Pennyrile, there is a well-known general store that hosts regular square dances for the local community and tourists passing through. This store is as much a community and cultural center as it is a place to purchase merchandise and also has rooms for guests to stay the night if the dance runs too late.

The only thing we know for sure about Rabbit Hash's name is that it actually wasn't called that at all when the town was founded. The original post office was established in 1879 as Carleton, Kentucky. Within about two months, the population and the postal service realized the name needed to be changed. There was too much confusion with Carrollton, Kentucky, just down the river.

According to one popular theory, the town was named for a popular meal after an abundance of rabbits fled to the hills during an Ohio River flood. Variations of the story say that it was named in response to two hungry travelers passing through during the flood, or that everyone ate rabbit for dinner one Christmas when the river was flooded. Another theory says that a boatman played a prank on the unsuspecting town doctor, inviting him over to dinner but serving the same rabbits the doctor had trapped himself. But these are all just theories.

We may never know how Rabbit Hash got its unique name, but Kentuckians who wind their way along the river to the Rabbit Hash Historic District agree that the general store is pretty special. Stop in for a cold Coca-Cola, groceries, or dry goods, if you need them, and snag a souvenir on your way out, too.

Rabbit Hash boasts a dog as its mayor and is home to this well-known general store that welcomes locals and visitors year round.

If you go to the Rabbit Hash General Store and you're really, truly lucky, you'll get to meet the mayor. She stops by the store at least once a day to check in on things, greet the townspeople, and welcome travelers passing through. You won't be able to shake her hand though…but maybe a paw? Did we mention the mayor is a dog?

Lucy Lou, the current mayor of Rabbit Hash, was elected in 2008 after the previous mayor, Junior, passed away. We weren't lucky enough to meet Lucy Lou during our visit. Hopefully, Lucy Lou will stick around as mayor for a good, long while, but when another Election Day comes, votes will cost you one dollar. You're welcome to vote as often as you'd like, too. Funds raised from the election go toward repairs and preservation for the historic district.

The Rabbit Hash General Store hosts a square dance each week for anyone who likes to cut a rug.

Just next door to the general store is the barn, and it's a pretty safe bet that there's probably a dance happening in the barn on any given night. Rabbit Hash pulls in bands from across the state and country. If the "Hashians" are partying during Old Timers Day, a parade, or really any halfway decent excuse for a celebration, you can bank on dancing in the barn.

And speaking of Old Timers Day, it is *the* big holiday around these parts. If you really want to see the full scope of what Rabbit Hash is all about, you'll want to be there on the Saturday of Labor Day Weekend. Plenty of musicians bring their instruments, townsfolk and tourists crowd the streets, and everyone enjoys food, music, and fun before Old Man Winter comes to town.

Aside from the locals—the last population count was 315 residents—Rabbit Hash is a popular stop for the Hash Hawgs and other bikers who enjoy riding the country roads of Boone County. The curving roads, the scenic views, and the friendly locals all make Rabbit Hash a prime destination for road warriors. You can mingle with the bikers talking mechanics on the front porch of the store or share a bite while enjoying the view of the Ohio River.

That was one of the best parts of our day in Rabbit Hash—kicking back with some good barbecue from the Scalded Hog and looking through the green trees at the town of Rising Sun, Indiana, across the water. We made a friend, too! A lovely fat local cat cozied up to us at the bar, begging for some of our barbecue.

The twin towns of Rabbit Hash and Rising Sun used to be a lot closer back in the day, socially speaking. During bitter cold winter days, the citizens would walk back and forth across the frozen river to visit friends, do business, or just to say they had.

Back in the early nineteenth century, Kentucky's border extended all the way to the low water mark on the other side of the Ohio River. That meant Kentuckians had control of the waterway, and businesses like Meek's Ferry sprung up at popular ports. The two towns grew up together, and the ferries played a big part in transporting goods between the growing populations and economies.

That's the real story about how the Rabbit Hash General Store became so integral to the community. A group of farmers originally built the structure to house their goods while waiting for the steamboats to arrive for commerce. Since the first manager and proprietor, James A. Wilson, opened for business in 1831, the Rabbit Hash General Store has been in continuous operation—more than 180 years. So come for a drive, stay for the dancing, and don't feed the mayor…she gets spoiled on human food.

If you go: Drive safe! Rabbit Hash can draw lots of folks on a warm summer's day. Curved roads and lots of walking traffic can make for a bad combo. Feel free to park pretty much anywhere, though. We were able to pull up on the side of the road just up from the Rabbit Hash General Store.

What it costs: Absolutely nothing, unless you want a drink or a meal or a Hash souvenir.

How to get there: Head up to Florence and pick up Kentucky 18 or U.S. 127 to Lower River Road. If you take U.S. 127, you'll pass by Big Bone Lick State Park. Maybe you want to make it a double header?

If you spend the weekend: The Old Hashienda, of course! It's a one-apartment inn in a converted historic building downtown. Check in at the general store and enjoy your stay in the rustic haven (with modern amenities).

9

A ROAD TRIP TO THE MONROE COUNTY MARBLE CLUB SUPER DOME

If you're in Tompkinsville on any given afternoon around four o'clock and you strain your ears down Armory Road, you'll hear the clacking of flint and the camaraderie of friendly competition. It's an old-fashioned marbles shootout, but don't mistake it for child's play. These are fierce competitors with their knees in the dirt and eyes focused beneath the brim of a ball cap. Friendly competitors, to be sure, but fierce nonetheless.

The men of the Marble Club Super Dome have been practicing and competing in "Rolley Hole"—as the official game is called—since the early 1900s; the super dome itself was built in the late 1980s. Different from a usual game of schoolyard marbles in much the same way chess differs from checkers, Rolley Hole is incredibly strategic. The court itself is fairly simple: a smooth, sifted dirt floor, about twenty feet by forty feet. A string marks out-of-bounds, and wooden boards along the sides prevent any rogue marbles from rolling off the playing ground. Three holes, each about half the depth of the marbles, sit along a centerline roughly eight feet apart. Teams of two compete against each other to try to block their opponents from landing marbles in the holes while at the same time trying to land their own marbles in those same holes three times, in order.

The court at the Monroe County Marble Club Super Dome has a big advantage: walls. Most marble courts are outdoors. Roofs shade the courts at Standing Stone State Park near Hilham, Tennessee, which hosts the national championship yearly. Though the super dome is a basic structure

Colonel Bowman is a founding member of the Monroe County Marble Club Super Dome. He is there each day at 4:00 p.m. to open the doors and to start a fire in the cold winter months. *Photo by Alix Mattingly.*

where architecture is concerned, an indoor facility with practice year-round is a huge asset. Teams from Kentucky dominate both national and international championships. The most widely publicized national championships in Kentucky are won in basketball, but one of the most dominant dynasties in the state resides in Monroe County with the men who practice and compete at the Marble Club Super Dome. The names of the champions are carved into a roof beam above the national championship court.

It's really amazing to hear the thwack! of a marble hitting another like a small gunshot. You have to have a strong thumb to shoot marbles, and some of the players in Monroe County can shoot the flint stones up to twelve feet away. Players' knees are always coated in dust and dirt from the floor of the dome; popular opinion states that you can always tell a marble player by the "click" of the stones in his or her pocket and the dirt embedded in his or her knee.

The marbles themselves are handmade with flint—sometimes agate—and durable. Any true player makes his or her own marbles using flint from nearby creeks, rivers, and lakebeds. They use diamond saws to cut the slabs into cubes, the edges of which are rounded off before being sanded into an absolutely smooth sphere. A *lot* of care is taken to measure and smooth marbles for competition. The stones must be weighted correctly and buffed to perfection to conform to championship rules and ensure a good roll. If you'd like to start practicing, yourself—you'll need about three to four marbles to start—you can buy them from 2012 national champion Paul Davis for twenty dollars apiece.

The founding members of the Monroe County club still come to shoot every evening. Colonel Bowman is generally the first one there, around 4:00 p.m., to open the doors and start a fire on cold days. The evenings tend to wrap up fairly early, around 8:00 p.m. or 8:30 p.m.; it is a farming community after all. And though you might think of a club as an insular and closed-off organization, the men of the super dome want to lend you a marble and teach you to shoot.

Most of these men, now fathers and some grandfathers, grew up playing the game. They're eager to pass the tradition along to younger generations and to expand the popularity of the sport. Some of the competitive pairs are father-son or grandfather-grandson combos. They run the club on custom and habit. There aren't any dues, but members of the community and the club donate each year for expenses and utilities.

The language is just as large a part of the culture as the game itself. Here are some terms you should know:

aggie: A marble made from agate.

allies: Sometimes used to describe a marble made of alabaster, but also used in place of "shooter" or "taw."

dog out: Rolling your marble to a better position to make a shot into the hole.

flintie: Flint marbles, also the hardest marbles in the sport. Flint marbles are only made in southern Kentucky and northern Tennessee.

plug: Tossing your shooter into the air toward the marbles on the court to make a play.

put English on it: To give the marble backspin.

shooter: Large marble used to knock other marbles around the court.

span: The distance between your thumb and pinkie when your hand is outstretched. Sometimes a player can move their shooter this distance forward during game play.

taw: Another term for "shooter," see above.

If you go: Be prepared to listen and learn. There's a lot of chatter (see some terms on the previous page) and rules to learn, but the club members are helpful and love to teach new players.

What it costs: Nothing. The super dome is free and there are no dues. You might want a marble of your very own, though. Those cost fifteen to twenty dollars.

How to get there: Head south on I-68 through Campbellsville, then pick up Kentucky 163 headed South just below the Cumberland Parkway. Once you're through Tompkinsville proper, head out Armory Road all the way to the end.

If you spend the weekend: The Tompkinsville Inn is your best bet for lodging, but you can also camp at Tompkinsville City Park.

FAMOUS SONGS ABOUT KENTUCKY

If you're traveling west along the Western Kentucky Parkway, you'll cross over the Green River just as you enter Muhlenberg County. To your left, settled down in the valley is the town of Paradise, mostly noted by locals for its paper mill and power plant that give off a rather pungent odor (seriously, the smell of a paper factory isn't pleasant). Paradise was the hometown of singer/songwriter John Prine's parents, and he spent a lot of time there as a young boy. That's why these song lyrics sound so familiar:

> *And daddy won't you take me back to Muhlenberg County*
> *Down by the Green River where Paradise lay*
> *Well, I'm sorry my son, but you're too late in asking*
> *Mister Peabody's coal train has hauled it away*

Mr. Peabody refers to the Peabody Coal Company, known today as Peabody Energy. Muhlenberg County was the home of Kentucky's first commercial coal mine. Usually, when folks think of coal, eastern Kentucky and Appalachia come to mind, but surface mining has been a popular industry in western Kentucky throughout the state's history. In fact, throughout the 1970s, Muhlenberg County was one of the leading sources of coal in the world. Prine obviously had a soured opinion of this controversial industry, as the second verse in his song reflects:

> *Then the coal company came with the world's largest shovel*
> *And they tortured the timber and stripped all the land*
> *Well, they dug for their coal till the land was forsaken*
> *Then they wrote it all down as the progress of man*

Prine wasn't the only Kentuckian to write a song about the Bluegrass State. Award-winning artist Loretta Lynn famously comes from "a cabin on a hill in Butcher Holler." Her song "Coal Miner's Daughter" became an Academy Award–winning film in 1980, and it paints a more nostalgic view of a coal mining town than Prine's track.

> *Yeah, I'm proud to be a coal miner's daughter*
> *I remember well the well where I drew water*
> *The work we done was hard*
> *At night we'd sleep 'cause we were tired*
> *I never thought of ever leaving Butcher Holler*

Kentucky's culture and tradition—and its fairer sex—lend themselves to many classic songs including "Blue Moon of Kentucky," a bluegrass music hit by Bill Monroe; "Kentucky Rain," performed by the one and only Elvis Presley and written by Eddie Rabbitt and Dick Heard; and Neil Diamond's "Kentucky Woman," written and recorded by the artist in 1967.

> *Kentucky woman*
> *She shines with her own kind of light*
> *She'd look at you once*
> *And a day that's all wrong looks alright*
> *And I love her, God knows, I love her*

And the country music duo Sundy Best honor their Kentucky roots in nearly all of their songs, perhaps most thoroughly in their ode to the

Mountain Parkway (the gateway into Appalachia) in their song "Mountain Parkway" or their homage to their roots in Prestonsburg in their single "Home" (part of the lyrics of this song follow).

Well I was born here in Kentucky
It's where my soul will rest in peace
I've been all around this world
There's no place that I'd rather be

10

A ROAD TRIP TO CAVE CITY

I t is a truth nearly universally acknowledged that the best discoveries you will make on a road trip are those that you don't plan for at all. All of the motorists who stumble onto the Olde Gener'l Store in Cave City most certainly know this to be true. Tucked away in a town packed full of eye-catching attractions and in the shadow of Guntown Mountain, it says a lot about this general store that it is one of the first things you'll see when you hop off I-65 at Exit 53.

Nestled right along this major thoroughfare that transports travelers through the southeast and up into the northern states, Cave City in Barren County could have easily become just another stop for gas on the way to another destination. It could have also become just another town you pass through on your way to Kentucky's only national park, Mammoth Cave. But Cave City capitalized on its unique citizens and key location and became a town full of must-see destinations like the Olde Gener'l Store.

So stuffed full of treasures that they are overflowing onto the store's wraparound porch and into the parking lot, no road tripper can be expected to pass by without stopping to explore. Signs lining the road leading up to the store declare it "The Most Unusual Store in Cave Country." It is certainly the most wonderful. The owner, Leroy, said his store has antiques, collector items, gifts, crafts, and other old "things and stuff" that he has been collecting for more than fifty years. This is a perfect description. If you're in Cave City—as your destination or on your way to somewhere else—stop by Leroy's store, and let him tell you his stories about finding old mirrors, bikes, and wagon wheels tucked away in friends' garages or about the time he bought twenty-two thousand license plates from the Kentucky State Penitentiary in 1976 right before the prisoners stopped making them by hand. You need an Elvis bust that was bought at an estate auction down the road. You must swoon over the paintings, vintage trucks and furniture, chandeliers, cast-iron treasures, and fully functional slot machine.

Leroy's Olde Gener'l Store in Cave City is the best place to find everything you never knew you always wanted.

You won't regret experiencing this man's collection and appreciating all the adventures he had finding his things and stuff.

After you stock up at the Olde Gener'l Store, take a quick drive down Mammoth Cave Road to one of the most creative, unique, and bizarre experiences you can have in Kentucky. You can see them from the road: a family of large woolly mammoths and a ginormous *Tyrannosaurus rex* welcoming you to Dinosaur World. Whether you've been driving past the sign (and the giant bright orange, scaly, prehistoric monster holding it) for years and never thought to stop or this is the first you're hearing of this gem, you're going to get a kick out of Dinosaur World.

Much like a wonderful day at the zoo, follow the mapped route through the park past the dinosaurs in their habitats with markers along the way giving you a bit of history and facts about each species. Raptors pop out at you from behind the bushes, the gentler-looking stegosaurus lounges next to a tree, and pterodactyls soar among the leaves. A quick detour takes you to the Mammoth Garden and a close-up bonding experience with your T. rex friend that resides next to I-65. Either before or after your walk through the Jurassic period, you can dig up fossils in the sand, uncover a dinosaur skeleton in the bone yard, and learn more about the time of the dinosaurs in the museum. Dinosaur World imagines what the

Dinosaur World in Cave City invites visitors to walk through a prehistoric zoo.

prehistoric creatures really looked like, and it gives visitors a glimpse of a world where they walk among the extinct. Kentucky is always doing the impossible.

If you go: Have an open mind and be ready to experience some of the most quirky tourist attractions around. Stop at every place that looks interesting to you. The Olde Gener'l Store is open every day but Sunday from 10 a.m. to close, which means whenever the shop is empty and Leroy feels like going home. Dinosaur World is open every day but Thanksgiving and Christmas.

What it costs: The Olde Gener'l Store doesn't cost a dime to walk around and have a look. But consider it a dare to leave there without something you just have to have. Prices on treasures vary dramatically but are fair. For the most up-to-date admission fees into Dinosaur World, visit www.dinosaurworld.com/kentucky.

How to get there: Take exit 53 from I-65 and head toward Mammoth Cave National Park on Mammoth Cave Road. The Olde Gener'l Store is located at 802 Mammoth Cave Road, and Dinosaur World is visible from the interstate.

If you spend the weekend: Spend a weekend in Cave City in style. Visit Mammoth Cave National Park, pick up some treasures from Leroy, visit the colorful dinosaurs, zipline down Guntown Mountain, and stay the night in a wigwam. You'll be telling stories about your trip for years to come.

WIGWAM VILLAGE NO. 2

Let's face it: Cave City, Kentucky, is not the same as New York City or Paris, France. You won't find a Ritz Carlton here or the Hotel Crillon but don't despair, Wigwam Village No. 2 is available for all your sleeping needs.

More than seventy-five years old, Wigwam Village No. 2 in Cave City was the dream of Frank A. Redford. Frank, inspired by a trip to a Sioux Reservation in South Dakota and a popular ice cream shop shaped like an upside down ice cream cone, finished construction on Wigwam Village No. 1 in Horse Cave, Kentucky, in 1935. He was so thrilled with the outcome that he patented his design in 1936 and built six more villages across the United States. Of the seven original Wigwam Villages, only three remain today: No. 2 in Cave City; No. 6 in Holbrook, Arizona; and No. 7 in Riallto, California.

The Wigwam Village may look a little familiar to you. Not only was Frank's Wigwam Motel franchise the inspiration for the Cozy Cone Motel in the Disney/Pixar film *Cars* (2006), but the queen of television herself Oprah Winfrey and her steadfast BFF Gayle King stayed in Wigwam Village No. 6 in Arizona during "Oprah and Gayle's Big Adventure." They were not quite as keen on the accommodations as we were.

Wigwam Village No. 2 is open year round and nightly rates vary based on season and day of the week. We stayed on a Saturday night in late March and paid fifty-five dollars for the night—a little over sixty dollars

Wigwam Village No. 2 in Cave City, seen here in 1940, is a quirky alternative to a traditional hotel. *Courtesy of the Library of Congress.*

after sales tax. It's more expensive in the summer months and on the weekends, but you aren't going to pay more than sixty dollars per night for one double bed and seventy dollars per night for two double beds.

11

A ROAD TRIP TO MAMMOTH CAVE NATIONAL PARK

Early cave guide Stephen Bishop called Mammoth Cave a "grand, gloomy, and peculiar place." While it may be all of those things—with its 392 miles of passageways and complex labyrinths, caverns, and vast chambers—there is really no other way to describe the cave than "mammoth."

The history of Mammoth Cave is long and complex. Credit for the cave's discovery ultimately belongs to natives of the land who lived here long before the state of Kentucky was ever thought of. However, Europeans have been claiming and reclaiming the cave for centuries. According to legend, at the turn of the nineteenth century, a bear chased John Houchins right into the entrance, earning him credit for the modern discovery of Mammoth Cave, unofficially. The first record of the cave is listed in the *Warren County Survey Book, 1796–1815*, naming Valentine Simon as the cave's first legal owner and stating that Simon "enters 200 acres of second rate land in Warren County by virtue of the Commissioner's Certificate No. 2428 lying on Green River beginning on a sycamore tree on the bank of said River thence running southward including two peter caves, thence angling down said river for quantity to include the improvement." Mammoth Cave was one of the two caves mentioned.

Later, in the 1920s, George Morrison could feel cool air coming out of the sinkhole he discovered miles away from the cave entrance previously explored by settlers in the area, and he knew there was a cave under his feet. So he did what any man in his position would do—he got some dynamite, stuck it inside the sinkhole and blew it up. Morrison had assumed correctly,

Mammoth Cave, located in Cave City, is the only national park in Kentucky.

and after he'd made the sinkhole a little bigger, he sent his nephew Earl down in the deep, dark unknown with a rope and a lantern (and, hopefully, a bit of a pep talk). Earl discovered a grand cave system, and after a little more exploration, he and Uncle George began giving tours of their cave and making a significant profit as the country was beginning to fall victim to the Great Depression. Ladies came down in their fanciest clothing, men dressed in shiny black shoes—all were eager to see Morrison's cave. Eventually, these guests began to get curious about what was deeper in the dark passageways that seemed to lead further underground. Morrison also wondered what was back there, so poor Earl was sent to find out. As it turned out, Mammoth Cave was back there, and just as the Great Depression was plaguing the United States, Morrison sold his cave to the existing Mammoth Cave owners for a chunk of change, and the new entrance of Mammoth Cave was established.

The New Entrance Tour of Mammoth Cave is one of many tours available at the national park. Be prepared, there are stairs involved—many, many stairs: 500 total on the two-hour tour, including 280 on your initial descent. On this tour, you'll enter the cave through a large metal door that leads to a staircase, which leads 250 feet under the surface of the Earth. That translates into lots of climbing, ducking, turning sideways, and squeezing

This "Old Entrance" to Mammoth Cave is the most popular corridor leading into this complex labyrinth underground cave system. The New Entrance was discovered in the 1920s.

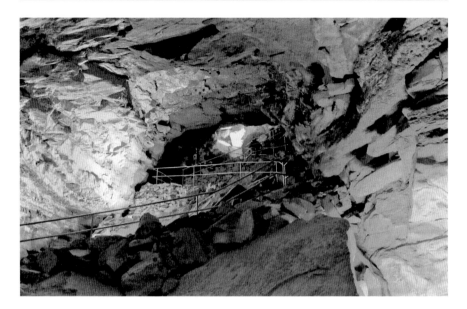

There are 392 miles of discovered cave passageways in Mammoth Cave National Park in Cave City.

through narrow passageways. And you know what they say, what goes down must go back up again, so be prepared to climb all of those stairs to get back to daylight. On this fairly brief tour, you'll travel a mere ¾ of a mile of the 392 total miles of Mammoth Cave, but it is a beautiful and very informative tour. You'll see stalactites and stalagmites (and learn the difference), and the very prepared tour guides will teach you all about these cave formations. Did you know it takes between three hundred and eight hundred years for one cubic inch of a stalactite to grow? That means the formations inside Mammoth Cave have been forming for thousands of years. Wrap your head around that.

Protect the bats: Depending on the year, there is a possibility that when you leave Mammoth Cave you're going to be required to walk across some squishy biosecurity mats covered in disinfectant. This is to prevent the spread of white-nose syndrome, which is not currently considered to be in Mammoth Cave, but the park is protecting its bats from the disease. What is white-nose syndrome? Basically, it's a fungus, new to North America, that has killed more than one million hibernating bats across the eastern United States since its discovery in 2006. It isn't harmful to humans, but you should still do your part to save the bats. If you aren't willing to walk across the mats, you won't be permitted into the cave. No exceptions.

If you go: The tours have some pretty strict rules (on direct orders from United States Homeland Security, of course), and you aren't allowed to take bags of any kind into the cave. If you take a camera, try not to drop it down any of the gaping holes you're going to pass and be mindful of the rest of your tour group when you use your flash. Also, keep in mind that when you enter the cave, you're essentially entering a dynamite-made-bigger sinkhole. You're descending several hundred feet under the Earth's surface into a natural space that was carved out by a waterway. You don't need to wear your bathing suit, but be prepared to walk through some puddles (be careful because the cave floor can get slick) and feel a few sprinkles from above. Finally, be prepared for your visit. You are going into a cave, which means it is going to be dark, it is going to be closed in (though most parts are very wide open with tall ceilings), and it's going to involve climbing and walking. Pack a light jacket and have fun!

What it costs: Tours range from five dollars to forty-eight dollars per person, depending on how big of an experience you want to have. The New Entrance Tour and Historic Tour are both twelve dollars and come highly recommended. The more expensive tours—such as the Wild Cave Tour—mean you're more than likely going to be in full spelunking gear, complete with hardhats and headlamps. Those cost more. Discounted rates are available to children and seniors. For more information on all tour prices as well as campground fees, visit the National Park Service website.

How to get there: Take I-65 to Cave City at Exit 53. Mammoth Cave Road will take you straight there.

If you spend the weekend: Get out and explore the rest of Cave City. You'll love its quirky tourist attractions.

 THE STORY OF FLOYD COLLINS

As far as famous Kentucky explorers go, most people think of Daniel Boone before they think of Floyd Collins. But Collins figures prominently, if infamously, in the pantheon of Bluegrass adventurers. A pioneer cave explorer, Collins became a national news sensation after he was trapped for two weeks while looking for a new entrance to the Mammoth Cave system.

In 1917, Collins discovered Crystal Cave—a lesser-known and more remote section of the Mammoth Cave system—managing it as a tourist attraction with his family. In a stroke of marketing genius, Floyd Collins decided he would begin searching for a new entrance to link the isolated Crystal Cave more closely to Mammoth Cave, thereby increasing tourism.

Working alone for more than three weeks on a neighbor's land that sat closer to the main roadway, Collins surveyed and enlarged a hole that would be dubbed "Sand Cave" by the national media. On January 30, 1925, Collins had been exploring several narrow passageways when his lamp began to die. In his hurry to leave the cave, several things happened: Collins got stuck in a narrow passage on his way out; he knocked his lamp over, leaving him in the dark; and in his fumbling, he dislodged a rock, which wedged his left leg between the closely spaced walls.

Floyd Collins was trapped, only 150 feet from the surface.

Friends discovered Collins the next day. They strung an electric light through the passageway and brought crackers to the immobilized explorer. For more than a week, Collins stayed trapped while rescuers tried to liberate him.

During this time, William Burke "Skeets" Miller, a young cub reporter from the *Louisville Courier-Journal*, was sent to cover the story of the man trapped in the cave. Miller's small stature enabled him to squeeze into the passageway himself, where he interviewed, prayed with, and brought food to Collins. Miller's daily stories were picked up quickly on the wire services, and soon, the entire nation was anxiously waiting to hear of Collins's successful rescue.

Then, the passage collapsed in two places.

Collins's rescuers began to dig a shaft to reach him from behind and release his leg from the wedged rock. But by the time they reached him, on February 17, Collins had died from hunger, thirst, and exposure. Funeral services were held at the surface of Sand Cave. Dissatisfied, Collins's brother, Homer, was able to reopen the shaft and recover Floyd's remains.

The tale of Floyd Collins became one of the largest news sensations in the interwar years (surpassed only by Charles Lindbergh's transatlantic flight and the kidnapping of Lindbergh's son). Miller's news stories from the scene of the almost-rescue earned him a Pulitzer Prize in 1926.

Both Crystal Cave and Sand Cave are now a part of Mammoth Cave National Park, though Crystal Cave is closed to visitors, and Sand Cave can only be explored from the surface.

In a more bizarre legacy, Collins's life and death inspired the award-winning off-Broadway musical *Floyd Collins*. The show, which first opened in 1996, has been performed across the United States and in the United Kingdom.

Some might look at Floyd Collins as a cautionary tale or a warning against exploring alone, but the tragic story of Floyd Collins ends with irony: Floyd had the right idea; Mammoth Cave does indeed pass beneath Sand Cave.

Visit these sources for additional information on the destinations and topics covered:

- *Kentucky State Parks: parks.ky.gov/parks/historicsites/jefferson-davis*
- *National Park Service: www.nps.gov*
- *United States Army at Fort Knox: www.knox.army.mil*
- *Pennyroyal Area Museum: www.museumsofhopkinsville.org/pam*
- *Kentucky Place Names by Robert Rennick (University Press of Kentucky, 1988)*
- *Rabbit Hash General Store: www.rabbithash.com*
- *Monroe County Tourism: www.monroecountykytourism.com/marble-super-dome.html*
- *Cave City Tourism: www.cavecity.com*
- *Dinosaur World: www.dinosaurworld.com/kentucky*
- *Wigwam Village: www.wigwamvillage.com*

- *National Park Service: www.nps.gov/maca/index.htm*
- *"Some Say the Bear Chased Houchins," National Park Service website, www.nps.gov/maca/historyculture/history2.htm*
- *"Not Black Gold, But Just as Good," National Park Service website, www.nps.gov/maca/historyculture/notblackgold.htm*

Part III
THE BLUEGRASS AND CENTRAL KENTUCKY

Some of Kentucky's most beautiful byways are in the Bluegrass Region, taking you through the rolling, green hills past horse farms, rock fences, and pastures. Make sure to follow the course of the Kentucky River to Frankfort and the grave of Daniel Boone. We all owe him a toast of bourbon as thanks for his pioneering spirit, without which we might never have called Kentucky home.

The Bluegrass Region is also where you can sail along the palisades of the Kentucky River, cliffs of the same limestone bedrock that's distilled with your bourbon and strengthens our Thoroughbred horses. The Bourbon Trail winds its way through most of the Bluegrass Region, taking you down scenic roadways to the distilleries that produce 95 percent of the world's bourbon. But please, designate a driver before you sample the goods.

You know that line in "My Old Kentucky Home": "The young folks roll on the little cabin floor"? You can visit both My Old Kentucky Home *and* the little cabin in the Bluegrass Region. We would have never been My Old Kentucky Road Trip without Stephen Collins Foster, and we'd like to think that the man who also wrote "Camptown Races" and "Oh, Susanna!" (even though he was actually from Pennsylvania) was our road trip spirit guide, bringing us only the best road trip tunes along the way.

12

A ROAD TRIP TO MY OLD KENTUCKY HOME

The sun always shines bright on this homestead named for a song that was inspired by it. This iconic state symbol encouraged the beginning of this road trip adventure, and it holds a special place in the hearts of many native Kentuckians who take pride in the state's history, traditions, culture, and unique attractions.

My Old Kentucky Home in Bardstown is actually Federal Hill, a former plantation built by United States senator John Rowan in 1795. The mansion was a meeting place for local politicians and often hosted visiting dignitaries, including Lexington's Henry Clay. The house is a beautiful but ultimately simple and classic Georgian-style home. Made of stone and brick native to the area, Federal Hill has two floors and a small attic, which include a dining room, a parlor, and four bedrooms. The home was passed down through generations of the family until Senator Rowan's granddaughter Madge Frost sold the mansion and accompanying 235 acres to the My Old Kentucky Home Commission, which renovated the property and gave the plantation to the state of Kentucky in 1922 for use as a state park.

Federal Hill is perhaps most famous for one guest in particular who is said to have stayed for some time in 1852. Kentuckians are confident—and who's going to say they're wrong—in this famous historical tie. The story goes that not-yet-famous songwriter Stephen Foster, a distant cousin of Senator Rowan, was inspired to pen "My Old Kentucky Home" after a stay at Federal Hill in 1852. Today, Foster is known for his hits "Oh! Susanna," "Camptown Races," "Jeanie with the Light Brown Hair," and

My Old Kentucky Home, which inspired the state song written by Stephen Foster after he visited relatives here, is located in Bardstown.

many others. "My Old Kentucky Home" was designated as the official state song in 1928, and Kentuckians have been tearing up every time it opens the Derby ever since.

Weep no more my lady
Oh weep no more today;
We will sing one song
For my old Kentucky home
For my old Kentucky home, far away

If you go: In addition to tours of the mansion, the state park also offers a gift shop, camping, and a golf course.

What it costs: Prices will vary between the cost of the tour, a showing of the Stephen Foster story, or special events like the My Old Kentucky Home Candlelight Tours. For detailed pricing information, visit the park's website at parks.ky.gov/parks/recreationparks/old-ky-home.

How to get there: Take Bluegrass Parkway to Bardstown and exit at U.S. 150. The state park is on your left. It is located at 501 East Stephen Foster Avenue. (The road is named after him, so he must have really stayed at Federal Hill!)

If you spend the weekend: See the famous *Stephen Foster Story* at the state park's amphitheater. Then, enjoy a few stops along the bourbon trail. What could be more Kentuckian than that?

Origins of Unique Kentucky Traditions

In a state commonly remembered for its Thoroughbred horseracing industry, famed Kentucky Derby, talented basketball teams and enthusiasm for bourbon, sometimes secret treasures go unnoticed.

During your adventure across the Bluegrass State, make sure you take some time to enjoy some of Kentucky's best-kept secrets:

The Hot Brown: This savory and creamy Kentucky delicacy was invented at Louisville's Brown Hotel by Fred K. Schmidt in 1926. The official story is that the chefs combined a couple traditional Welsh sandwiches to make an alternative to serving ham and egg for late-night suppers. But according to the tall tales of the locals, Schmidt invented this open-faced stack of turkey, bacon, Mornay sauce, and tomato by accident. The way the story goes, after a busier than usual evening at the Brown, Schmidt ran out of several ingredients in his kitchen and was unable to make the special that was featured on the menu that night. So he threw together everything he could find and plated it for guests. Visitors requested the dish every night from then on, and it was added to the hotel dining room's regular menu.

A mint julep: This bourbon cocktail is not exclusive to Kentucky, but it is at its best in the Bluegrass State. Nowhere is that more evident than at the Kentucky Derby. The mint julep has been the traditional beverage of Churchill Downs for almost a century. Each year, almost 120,000 mint juleps are served over the two-day period of the Kentucky Oaks and the Derby. It

A mint julep, the famed drink of the Kentucky Derby. *Photo via iStock.*

requires more than ten thousand bottles of bourbon, one thousand pounds of freshly harvested mint, and sixty thousand pounds of ice. Scale that down a bit for your next house party. You'll only need a julep cup of shaved ice, Kentucky bourbon, some homemade simple syrup (boil two cups of water and two cups of sugar together for five minutes), and a sprig of fresh mint.

Burgoo: Let's clear the air up front and list the most important basics about this Kentucky favorite right away: burgoo is not chili; it is not vegetable stew; and it is best cooked outside over an open fire in a cast-iron pot. Burgoo is traditionally made with whatever vegetables are in the kitchen and whatever meat is easily accessible. Venison, squirrel, opossum, raccoon, and game birds will work just fine. In Kentucky, we like to make the burgoo fixin' a social event. In the autumn, just when the weather starts to turn cold, invite all of your friends to bring an ingredient and build a fire. Y'all can share stories around the campfire while dinner cooks.

 ALL ABOUT BOURBON

I have never in my life seen a Kentuckian who didn't have a gun, a pack of cards, and a jug of whiskey.
—*Andrew Jackson*

We're not sure that the first two still apply, but as for the third, you'd be hard pressed to find a Kentucky home without a bottle of bourbon on a shelf *somewhere*. Bourbon is everywhere these days, and there are certain things every Kentuckian should know about our native spirit.

All bourbons are whiskeys, but not all whiskeys are bourbon. Bourbon distinguishes itself from whiskey in five key ways:
1. The mash bill, or recipe, must contain at least 51 percent corn.
2. Bourbon is distilled to no more than 160 proof, or 80 percent alcohol by volume (ABV).
3. Bourbon is aged in *new*, charred oak barrels. Fun fact: almost all of those barrels, once used, are sent to distilleries in Scotland to age their whiskeys.
4. It must enter the barrel for aging at no more than 125 proof, or 62.5 percent ABV.
5. It must be bottled at 80 proof (40 percent ABV) or higher.

Bourbon ages in barrels at Woodford Reserve Distillery in Versailles.

One of the most common misconceptions about the production of bourbon is the myth that the spirit can *only* be called bourbon if it is produced in Kentucky. In actuality, a bourbon can only be called "Kentucky Bourbon" if it is distilled in Kentucky, and 95 percent of all bourbon manufactured comes from the Bluegrass State. Our own personal belief is that the best bourbons—the bottles you want to drink—only come from Kentucky.

Drink Bourbon Like a Kentuckian

The truly classic recipe for Kentucky bourbon is "neat." Simple. Flavorful. Delicious—OK, maybe you can put a few ice cubes in there. If you want to experiment in mixology, here's an all-time favorite:

CLASSIC OLD-FASHIONED
(The hard way and the easy way)

Place a sugar cube in the bottom of an Old-Fashioned glass (or you can put a teaspoon of sugar in a thick-bottomed cocktail glass of your choosing). Moisten the sugar with a few dashes of Angostura bitters. It's easy to find bitters at just about any store that sells beverages. (For a bit more flavor, a lot of folks like to muddle a wedge of orange and a maraschino cherry in the bottom of a glass with the sugar and bitters, then add the other ingredients. If you don't have a muddler, the back of a spoon works great to crush some of the flavor from the fruit.) Drop in a few ice cubes and a splash of hot water (or soda water) and stir with a bar spoon (or a regular spoon, no need to be fancy on our account). Add bourbon. The precise bartender would call for two ounces. We call for whatever makes you happy and is to your taste. Bottoms up!

13

A ROAD TRIP TO DANIEL BOONE'S GRAVE SITE

Unless you're in the car with an older relative, it isn't exactly common to include a graveyard/cemetery/memorial garden on your road trip. But an exception should be made in the case of the Frankfort Cemetery, located just off of East Main Street headed into historic downtown Frankfort. This cemetery sits on a cliff overlooking the Kentucky River and the capitol building, but it isn't the beautiful sunsets that make it notable. Seventeen Kentucky governors, famed regional watercolorist Paul Sawyier, and trailblazing pioneer Daniel Boone and his wife, Rebecca, are among the notable residents of this graveyard.

While Boone is held in high regard nationally as an American pioneer, explorer, frontiersman, and folk hero, in Kentucky, he is held in even greater esteem for his settlement of the state.

An avid trapper and hunter, Boone had heard tale of the fertile land and abundant game that were across the Appalachian Mountains from Virginia. He first reached Kentucky in the fall of 1767, in what is present-day Elkhorn City. Boone returned to the state a few times before packing up his family in 1773 and attempting to establish a settlement in Kentucky with a very small group of immigrants. Boone played a key role in negotiations and treaties with the Shawnee, Cherokee and Delaware Native American tribes that lived in Kentucky.

Boone moved into what is now Missouri in 1799 and spent his final years there. He died in 1813 just before his eighty-sixth birthday. He was buried next to his wife, Rebecca, in an unmarked grave on Tuque Creek

Daniel Boone is buried with his wife, Rebecca, at the Frankfort Cemetery in Frankfort, overlooking the Kentucky River and the state capitol building.

in Missouri. In 1845, Daniel's and Rebecca's remains were moved to the cemetery in Frankfort.

This road trip is worth it for the views alone. Go at sunrise to see the sun's first light break over the capitol dome. Go at sunset and see the sun fall to the horizon behind the government buildings. Also take time to appreciate the rich history that is buried in the cemetery and the sacrifices that were made to establish this great state so many years ago.

If you go: Keep an eye out for wildlife. A few curious foxes have been spotted here.

What it costs: Not a thing, and the view is priceless.

How to get there: The cemetery is located on East Main Street in Frankfort, between downtown and Kentucky State University's campus. Pull in the gates of the cemetery and clearly marked signs will take you straight to Daniel and Rebecca Boone.

If you spend the weekend: There is so much to see and do in the state's capital! Book a room at the Capital Plaza Hotel and tour the capitol building, Rebecca Ruth Candy Factory, and Buffalo Trace Distillery, just to name a few.

FRANKFORT, KENTUCKY'S CAPITAL CITY

Kentucky's capital city was first settled in 1786. As the story goes, the town got its name after a group of Native Americans attacked a group of early American pioneers who were making salt at a ford in the Kentucky River. Pioneer Stephen Frank was killed, and settlers began calling the crossing Frank's Ford. And as many things in Kentucky get named, enough people mispronounced the name that it eventually became simply Frankfort.

The Kentucky River cuts through the middle of modern day Frankfort, which is home to Kentucky State University, the state's only historically black college and university and one of two land-grant institutions in the state. The city is full of historic sites, museums, restored mansions, unique attractions, and bourbon. On your way through this picturesque town, make sure you stop to see these top destinations:

The Kentucky State Capitol Building: This capitol building is the fourth governing location since statehood in 1792. The current structure replaced the earlier 1830 capital, which still stands in downtown Frankfort. This capitol was built to accommodate an expanding state government. Ground broke on the building in 1904, and the project was completed and dedicated in 1910. The exterior of the building is faced in Indiana limestone and Vermont granite. The sculptured pediment of the classical front portico depicts allegorical figures that represent Kentucky—the central female figure, with Progress, History, Plenty, Law, Art, and Labor as her attendants. Guided tours are available Monday through Friday from 8:30 a.m. to 3:00 p.m.

View of the state capitol building from Frankfort Cemetery.

The Floral Clock: This thirty-four-foot garden landmark stands behind the capitol building and was constructed in the 1960s as a joint project between state government and the Garden Club of Kentucky. The clock weighs about five hundred pounds, and its face is composed of more than ten thousand flowers, mostly begonias. All of the flowers used in the clock face are grown in local greenhouses. The clock is suspended above a round pool of water that visitors often use as a wishing well. Money collected from the pool is used for state scholarships.

Frankfort Cemetery: One of the best parts about Frankfort is that there are beautiful views tucked around every corner and over the top of every hill, even in the places you least expect to find them. This cemetery sits on top of a cliff overlooking the Kentucky River, the state capitol and governor's mansion, and downtown Frankfort. Seventeen Kentucky governors; trailblazing pioneer Daniel Boone and his wife, Rebecca; and famed regional watercolorist Paul Sawyier are buried here.

Rebecca Ruth Candy: This Frankfort candy company, founded in 1919, claims to have invented the regionally famous Bourbon Ball candy. Friends and former teachers Rebecca Gooch and Ruth Hanly Booe first got the

City of Frankfort, Kentucky's state capital.

idea of mixing candy and bourbon together at Frankfort's sesquicentennial celebration in 1936 on the suggestion of dignitary Eleanor Hume Offutt. Ruth worked on the recipe for two years before perfecting the still secret process. Tours of this candy factory are available.

Buffalo Trace Distillery: The smell of mash often floats in the air throughout Frankfort's east side because of this two-hundred-year-old distillery. Formerly known as the George T. Stagg Distillery and the O.F.C. Distillery, Buffalo Trace is the oldest continuously operating distillery in America. It is named for its location on land where buffalo used to cross the Kentucky River.

Buckley Wildlife Sanctuary: This 374-acre natural sanctuary along the Kentucky River includes fifty acres of fields and two ponds surrounded by mixed-mesophytic forest. Managed by the Life Adventure Center, Buckley Wildlife encourages visitors and provides an active educational program.

Goldenrod, the Kentucky state flower, through fence boards at sunset.

Thoroughbred horses on a farm in Lexington, the Horse Capital of the World.

A hiking trail in Red River Gorge.

The state capitol building sitting on the Kentucky River in Frankfort.

Thoroughbreds race during the Fall Meet at Keeneland Race Track in Lexington.

Morning fog in Red River Gorge.

Above: Bourbon barrels aging at the Woodford Reserve Distillery in Versailles.

Right: Raccoons before sunrise on a central Kentucky farm.

Opposite, top: Spring flowers in Kentucky.

Opposite, bottom: Morning fog settled over the Kentucky River.

A waterfall on Bark Camp Creek in Kentucky at the beginning of autumn.

Cumberland Falls in autumn.

Young Thoroughbred horses playing on a central Kentucky farm.

A moonbow at Cumberland Falls.

A buck during Kentucky's hunting season.

A waterfall on Hickman Creek in autumn.

Opposite, top: Red River Gorge in the fall.

Opposite, middle: Thoroughbred horses at sunset in central Kentucky.

Opposite, bottom: A Civil War reenactor at the battle of Perryville.

Snow falls in winter at a waterfall in Red River Gorge.

Fireflies on a Kentucky summer night.

Opposite, top: Gingko leaves on a hiking trail in Daniel Boone National Forest.

Opposite, bottom: The Kentucky River at the Palisades.

A foggy western Kentucky sunrise.

Sunrise over Maysville, Kentucky.

Opposite, top: A spider web collects morning dew.

Opposite, bottom: A fox at the Frankfort Cemetery.

A Kentucky farm at sunrise.

Natural Bridge State Resort Park.

The sun sets behind a western Kentucky barn.

The sun rises over the Ohio River from Kentucky's banks at Maysville.

The sun sets over the Abbey of Gethsemani.

A summer storm rolls in over a central Kentucky farm.

14

A ROAD TRIP TO LEXINGTON

We started this road trip because we've lived in Kentucky our whole lives and have barely scratched the surface of all there is to see and do. The same holds true for the city we grew up in. We were both born and raised in Lexington, and while we personally consider ourselves experts on the town, it turned out to be not the least bit true.

Whether you're interested in beautiful Thoroughbred horse farms (with barns bigger and more luxurious than your homes, no joke), history (you can visit the homes of Henry Clay, Mary Todd Lincoln, John Wesley Hunt, and Confederate president Jefferson Davis) or outdoor adventures (visit the University of Kentucky's arboretum or McConnell Springs), there's always something going on in Lexington. Even when it isn't basketball season.

We'll start with some quick facts:

- Lexington was founded in June 1775 in what was then Virginia, seventeen years before Kentucky became a state in 1792.
- The first American performance of a Beethoven symphony was in Lexington in 1817.
- The brass plate embedded in the sidewalk at the corner of Limestone and Main Streets in downtown Lexington is a memorial marker honoring Smiley Pete, known as the town dog. He died in 1957.
- The Jif plant in Lexington is the largest peanut butter–producing facility in the world. On warm summer days, you can smell the roasting peanuts several miles away from the factory.

- The great Man O' War racehorse—who was born on Lexington's Nursery Stud farm on March 29, 1917—won all of his horse races except one, which he lost to a horse named Upset.

One of our favorite spots in Lexington is a bit of green space two blocks north of Main Street between Transylvania University and West Second Street. Originally dedicated as Centennial Park in 1876, Gratz Park was renamed for Benjamin Gratz, a prominent hemp grower who made his home among the Federal and Greek Revival homes surrounding the park. And trust us, if ever you win the lottery, you'll want to buy one of these houses—beautiful architecture in Lexington's first historic district and only two blocks away from downtown restaurants, shops, and bars (which serve bourbon, of course).

Between the historic homes, the mirrored facades of Transylvania University and the former Carnegie Library (now the Carnegie Center for Literacy and Learning), the views of the Lexington skyline, and the peace and quiet, Gratz Park is one of the most tranquil settings in town.

You'll be amazed at just how much history is in a one-block radius. Standing in the middle of the park, you can see the oldest University west of the Allegheny Mountains, Lexington's first public library, the Hunt-Morgan House, the birthplace of the Lexington Clinic, the headquarters for both the Union and Confederate armies during the Civil War, and the home of the founder of the *Lexington Leader* newspaper (later merged with the *Lexington Herald* to create the *Lexington Herald-Leader*).

The Hunt-Morgan house, which sits just on the edge of Gratz Park, was home to some of Lexington's biggest (and often overlooked) historical figures. Here's the family story: John Wesley Hunt, the first millionaire west of the Alleghenies built the house in 1814—$1 million in 1814 is worth almost $13 million today. His son, Charlton, became the first mayor of Lexington. His grandson John Hunt Morgan was the famous Confederate Civil War general known as the "Thunderbolt of the Confederacy" who led Morgan's Raid in 1863. The story all the locals remember was his leap over the garden's brick wall on horseback to kiss his mother goodbye. John Wesley Hunt's great-grandson was Dr. Thomas Hunt Morgan, born in 1866. His pioneering work in genetics earned him a Nobel Prize in Physiology or Medicine in 1933.

Elsewhere in downtown, on the southwest corner of South Mill and West Main Streets, is where the settling of Lexington began. A blockhouse was built in 1779 and eventually was expanded into a fort that stood largely between South Mill and South Broadway Streets on West Main. The

Downtown Lexington, sometimes called the Athens of the West for its diverse arts and culture.

northern edge of the fort stopped in the middle of what is now West Main Street. Across the street from this intersection stands the tallest building in Lexington, the 5/3 Bank building—or "Big Blue Building" as the locals call it.

If you're standing in front of the Big Blue Building and looking across Main Street, you'll have a full view of the old courthouse and Cheapside Park. It's common to see people enjoying lunch at one of the cafés or restaurants that border Cheapside or lounging around on outdoor patios. In the evenings, locals walk their dogs on the lawn of the old courthouse, and on summer nights, bands play on the pavilion stage. It is most certainly a different scene than what history tells us about Cheapside more than a century ago.

During the era of slavery, the lawn of Lexington's courthouse was one of the largest slave markets in the state. According to historical documents, slaves were auctioned and sold in the courtyard that stands between today's West Main and West Short Streets in front of the old courthouse building. The healthier and younger slaves, considered to be more suited for work, were auctioned on one side of the lawn while the slaves who were older or had health problems were auctioned on the other side. The latter was dubbed "the cheap side." And while the history of the origin has faded and slaves have long been absent from the courthouse lawn, the name stuck.

Horses play on one of Lexington's many Thoroughbred horse farms. Lexington is known as the Horse Capital of the World.

The courthouse that stands next to Cheapside Park is no longer a working courthouse but now a museum and office space. The current Lexington Circuit and District Courts are located a few blocks to the east of this site.

Other don't-miss places and activities in Lexington include:

- Watch an early morning workout or a race at Keeneland Race Course or the Red Mile Harness Track. Keeneland meets take place in October and April; Standardbred racing happens at Red Mile between August and October.
- For more horses, head out to the Kentucky Horse Park to see champions grazing, learn about various breeds, and walk through the trophy room to see Secretariat's Derby trophy on display.
- Take a walk through historic (and beautiful) Lexington Cemetery, the final resting place of Henry Clay, General John Hunt Morgan, Adolph Rupp, and other famous Lexingtonians.
- Pass the time watching the Foucault pendulum swing at the Lexington Public Library's Central Branch. It's the world's largest ceiling clock.
- Float your car across the Kentucky River at the Valley View Ferry, the oldest year-round ferry operating in the United States. But call before you go; high water conditions mean the ferry won't be running.

If you go: Make sure it's for a few days, so you can fit in every piece of unique culture the Athens of the West has to offer.

What it costs: Well that depends on what you want to do. But the greatest thing about Lexington is how affordable it is and how many things are free to just walk around. If you're concerned about cost, call ahead to each destination before you start your trip.

How to get there: Located in the middle of central Kentucky's Bluegrass Region, Lexington is at the crossroads of Interstates 75 and 64 and is a beginning point for the Bluegrass Parkway. U. S. 68 also runs right through the middle of town.

If you spend the weekend: A whole weekend? What a fabulous idea. Lexington is a central location for a lot of really cool day trips, but make sure you explore everything Horse Country has to offer before venturing on to other Kentucky destinations. Nearby attractions include Shaker Village of Pleasant Hill, the Kentucky Bourbon Trail, and the Lake Herrington marinas.

WHAT MAKES BLUEGRASS BLUE?

It is a common misconception of visitors to the Bluegrass State that as soon as they cross the state line, those rolling acres of bright green grass are going to turn, well, blue. It is a silly notion to the natives, but to be fair, it makes sense. In a state that has been known to "Bleed Blue" on many occasions and that proudly declares itself the Bluegrass State, it's a reasonable assumption that the grass might really be that color.

Just to be clear: it isn't blue. It is green, just like everywhere else. Bluegrass, or *Poa pratensis*, is a type of grass seed that is incredibly common in North America and found in many places outside of Kentucky. Contrary to many stories, it isn't Kentucky's famous limestone or granite that gives the grass a hint of azure, anil, or topaz. And it isn't named for its leaves, which stay green year round. This grass is named for its seed heads, which appear during the

Central Kentucky is known for its bluegrass, and Kentucky is the Bluegrass State, but the grass is still green. The seeds on naturally growing fields of bluegrass make the ground covering appear blue, especially when coated in early morning dew.

spring and summer when the grass is allowed to grow unshorn to a natural height of one to three feet. An unmown field of seeding *Poa pratensis* waving in a summer breeze is undeniably blue. And in Kentucky, rolling expanses of untouched fields shining in the morning dew give the state its moniker of the Bluegrass State.

 THE VERSAILLES ROAD CASTLE

The rolling hills of bluegrass and picturesque Thoroughbred horse farms that line the road connecting Versailles and Lexington are the same beautiful and iconic images of central Kentucky you'll find on postcards at local gift stores. But it isn't these charming views that cause traffic to noticeably slow down as you top the last hill before entering Fayette County, it is the stone turrets that come into view. If the Bluegrass region's green hills didn't already resemble the landscapes of western Europe and the United Kingdom, the

CastlePost in Versailles is a local legend and known in the area as the Versailles Road Castle.

stone walls, turrets, and drawbridge of Castle Post, known locally as simply the Castle or the Versailles Road Castle—or sometimes Martin Castle, for its previous owners—certainly give the feeling that you've traveled across the Atlantic, or even back in time.

As far as neighbors can determine, this castle is void of any knights in shining armor, and the clusters of people standing outside its gates are tourists taking pictures, not villagers arriving for market. And while this Versailles castle's history isn't as rich (literally or figuratively) as its counterpart in France, sordid rumors of its past are nearly as entertaining.

First and foremost, the castle began as a labor of love. Rex and Caroline Martin were taken with old European castles they saw while on vacation in 1968. When they returned home, they purchased fifty-three acres off U.S. 60 in Woodford County just outside of Lexington and broke ground on their dream home in 1969. The Martins' finished estate was to have seven bedrooms, fifteen baths, four corner towers, a dozen turrets, 12-foot-high walls, a drawbridge, an Italian fountain in the courtyard, and tennis courts out back. But before the castle could be completed, the couple divorced, and Rex stopped building, leaving the 10,400-square-foot, two-story home unfinished and empty.

In 1988, Rex put his castle on the market with a For Sale sign posted on the gates that announced showings by appointment only. The castle was up for sale on and off for the better part of two decades, but as the story goes, countless real estate agents who showed interest in the property never received any response from Rex.

Rex died in 2003 without ever selling the castle. Later that year, Thomas Post, a graduate of Lexington's Lafayette High School and the University of Kentucky, bought the property for $1.8 million and announced plans to convert the castle into a bed-and-breakfast so that locals and tourists would finally have an opportunity to peek behind walls they'd been speculating about for years. But in 2004, the house inside those gates caught fire, burning nearly the entire main building to the ground. Locals who caught wind of the fire gathered along Versailles Road late into the night as the iconic structure went up in flames.

The new owner rebuilt, completing construction in 2008. Today, the castle is a luxury hotel and event venue, boasting rooms ranging from $195 to $420 per night. Inside, a great hall with thirty-foot ceilings, solid stone walls, and elegant chandeliers welcome guests. The castle also includes a library, a large dining room, a gourmet kitchen, a sun-lit breakfast room, and twelve extravagant suites. CastlePost is located at 230 Pisgah Pike in Versailles.

15

A ROAD TRIP TO THE PERRYVILLE BATTLEFIELD

When the first battles of the Civil War broke out in April 1861, ladies and their gentlemen brought picnic lunches and sociability to the edges of the battlefield. However, as the casualties mounted on both sides, the spectators quickly realized the war was no Sunday afternoon frivolity. Luckily for us, the reenactment of the battle of Perryville is. And yes, you can bring a picnic lunch.

The battle of Perryville, fought on October 8, 1862, was one of the bloodiest of the Civil War and is the largest battle fought on Kentucky soil. The battle lasted approximately six hours, more than 1,400 men were killed, more than 5,500 were wounded, and almost 1,200 men were captured or missing. Kentucky played host to several other skirmishes thanks to its border-state status, including the battle of Mill Springs, the battles at Forts Donelson and Henry, General John Hunt Morgan's infamous raids, the battle of Munfordville, and the battle of Paducah. As a border-state, Kentucky was a key to the strategies of the Union and the Confederacy. Lincoln was quoted, "I hope to have God on my side, but I must have Kentucky" and "I think to lose Kentucky is nearly the same as to lose the whole game...We would as well consent to separation at once, including the surrender of the capital." The state's position along the Ohio and Mississippi Rivers made the successful occupation of Kentucky by either army a tactical advantage. In 1862, the Confederates launched their Kentucky Campaign, pushing north from Tennessee.

Though the Confederates were victorious that day in Perryville, the Southerners were outnumbered and forced to withdraw. Eventually,

Civil War reenactors travel from across the country to take part in the recreation of the battle of Perryville each year.

the Confederacy also had to give up on Kentucky, and the tide of war turned, allowing President Lincoln enough leverage to sign the Emancipation Proclamation.

If you go: If you're not a fan of loud, percussive noises; walking; or the milling about of large family groups, going to the reenactment is not for you. If, however, you enjoy action, interaction and history, you're going to love it! The reenactment usually features about seventy-five reenactors from the Sixth Ohio Volunteer Infantry reenacting company, based out of Cincinnati, Ohio. We chatted with one of the Union men, and he told us they participate in approximately two reenactments per month during the summer (high-season for reenactments) and visit plenty more.

What it costs: Going to the reenactment will cost you ten dollars per car, more for passenger vans and buses. There are a few add-ons at the state historic site as well, such as a Guided Battlefield Tour (five dollars per person) and the Ghosts of Perryville Tour (ten dollars per person led by SHOCK, the Spirit Hunters of Central Kentucky).

How to get there: From Lexington, take U.S. 68 South to Kentucky 1920. The programming information for the reenactment warned us to beware of traffic congestion and troubles parking, but we didn't have any troubles at all. Perhaps it was the virtue of a Sunday afternoon, but we made it to Perryville quickly and easily, and the uniformed attendant guided us straight to parking.

A few more notes:

- The battlefield is big. And not only is the battlefield big, but the entirety of the Perryville State Historic Site is big. The soldiers at the actual battle of Perryville had trouble navigating the terrain, and you will too if you don't wear good walking shoes. Heck, you might have trouble if you do wear good walking shoes; we had a bit of trouble walking sideways across the hills, up the hills, and down the hills. But it really does make you appreciate just how easily an entire army might sneak up on you from atop a ridge.
- We had a beautiful day to watch the reenactment—warm in the sunshine, cool and breezy in the shade. But, as we all know, Kentucky weather is notoriously fickle, and the battle will go off whether it's sunny, raining, or snowing. The reenactors this year had to spend the night in below forty-degree temperatures in their Civil War camps and the battle itself was fought during one of the worst droughts in Kentucky history, so be prepared.
- On that note, you may also want to bring a chair. Some of the folks had picnic blankets and stadium chairs and a great vantage point to watch from. Bear in mind, however, you will be dragging that chair with you everywhere you roam across the park.
- If you're easily startled by loud noises, here's your warning: there are guns and cannons, and they make loud, startling noises. When the cannon went off the first time, there wasn't a single person in the crowd who didn't yelp or jump. And when the cannon kept going off, people continued to be startled by it, along with their pets.

Reenactors at the Perryville Battlefield.

- Which brings us to another note: yes, you can bring your friendly dog, but there are lots of horses and children running around and loud noises, so it might be wise to bring your dog only if he or she has a Zen-like demeanor and wonderful social skills.

Interacting with the reenactors: The best part about going to a Civil War battle reenactment is interacting with the reenactors—say that five times fast. We chatted with a few fellas from the Union company, one of whom was clearly brave because he let us aim his rifle! The reenactors want you to come talk to them and ask lots of questions, and they really know their stuff. They can tell you all about how the soldiers lived, trained and fought; what their families were doing back home; and plenty of other great historical and cultural tidbits from the 1860s. You can check out the camps they set up (and, yes, live in during the reenactments) and shop for re-creations of artifacts from the time period.

16

A ROAD TRIP TO SHAKER VILLAGE AND THE KENTUCKY RIVER PALISADES

'Tis the gift to be simple, 'tis the gift to be free
'Tis the gift to come down where we ought to be,
And when we find ourselves in the place just right,
'Twill be in the valley of love and delight.
When true simplicity is gained,
To bow and to bend we shan't be ashamed,
To turn, turn will be our delight,
Till by turning, turning we come 'round right.
—Simple Gifts by Elder Joseph Brackett, 1848

In sharp contrast to our harried, busy and technology-filled culture, Shaker Village of Pleasant Hill is a sanctuary for the simple life. The Shaker community that flourished at Pleasant Hill near Harrodsburg, Kentucky, thrived for more than one hundred years.

The community got its start when three missionaries from the original Shaker settlement in New Lebanon, New York, made the trek to Kentucky and began proselytizing to citizens in the Bluegrass Region of Kentucky. Within eighteen months, forty-four Believers signed the first family covenant in Kentucky and moved their settlement to a hill in Mercer County with ample land and gorgeous views of the surrounding countryside that became Pleasant Hill.

Pleasant Hill and its congregation grew and prospered quickly. The operation picked up tracts of land surrounding the original settlement to

A spiral staircase crafted with no supports at Shaker Village of Pleasant Hill in Harrodsburg. The Shakers were well known for their architecture and sophisticated building techniques.

fill with crops and orchards. Sustainable agriculture practices and diligent productivity enabled them to trade surplus goods, crops and livestock up and down the Kentucky and Ohio Rivers.

Eventually, Pleasant Hill grew to around five hundred Believers and more than 260 structures, though fewer than 40 remain. But almost as quickly as the Shakers established themselves in Kentucky, industrialization began sweeping through the United States, bringing change of all kinds but especially a shift from rural to urban culture. The Shaker community, whose belief in celibacy only allowed their community to grow through conversion, began to deplete. The Civil War and ensuing Reconstruction period further consumed resources and potential converts.

In 1910, the twelve remaining members of the community deeded the land and structures to a local merchant who cared for the community until the last member passed away in 1923. Owned by private hands, the village operated as "Shakertown" until restoration began several decades later.

Shaker Village of Pleasant Hill in Harrodsburg.

Today, Shaker Village of Pleasant Hill is an opportunity to step back into history and simplicity. The nonprofit corporation works to preserve the remaining land and structures and educate visitors on the impact the Shaker community had on the state.

The most remarkable part of visiting Shaker Village of Pleasant Hill is the authentic way the employees maintain the village. Fields and livestock are tended using primitive agricultural methods; artists and artisans craft goods such as brooms, pottery, and farming and cooking implements in the workshops on site; and native plant and animal species live in the nature preserve.

If you go: It takes at least a full day to fully appreciate all that Shaker Village of Pleasant Hill has to offer. One of our favorite activities is cruising down the Kentucky River on the Dixie Belle riverboat. Embark at Shaker Village Landing (a ticket will cost you ten dollars), and spend an hour cruising down the Kentucky River between the famous and picturesque palisades. The Captains Herring, a team of brothers who operate the Dixie Belle, take you from the dock, under High Bridge (the most aptly named structure if there ever

The *Dixie Belle*, a riverboat at Shaker Landing at Shaker Village of Pleasant Hill in Harrodsburg.

The *Dixie Belle* takes visitors up the Kentucky River to see the palisades and discusses the history of the Shaker people and of the river.

was one) and downstream, all while pointing out the river's diverse ecosystem. Before you head down to the landing, make sure the brakes on your car are in working order; the hill down to the river is steep. Make sure you're there after lunch to catch the first boat at 1:00 p.m.

The rest of your day at Pleasant Hill can be spent hiking along the forty-mile trail system, exploring the history and operations of the original village, shopping for Shaker-style crafts or dining at the inn. And speaking of the inn…

What it costs: Costs can add up a bit if you're adding tickets on to a stay in the inn and meals in the dining room. If you're just going for the day, it's absolutely free to drive through the grounds and walk along the hiking trails. Tours of the village cost fifteen dollars for adults, with discounted evening rates, and five dollars for six- to twelve-year-old children. The Dixie Belle riverboat is an additional ten dollars for adults, five dollars for six to twelve-year-old children and free for children five and under. Weekend wagon rides during the summer and fall months are six dollars for anyone six years or older.

As for meals and lodging, menus vary for lunch and dinner and by season. Be sure to make a reservation before you go. Call for nightly rates at the inn for your selected dates: 800-734-5611.

How to get there: From Lexington, follow Harrodsburg Road (U.S. 68) west for about twenty-five miles.

If you spend the weekend: The best place to stay for your Pleasant Hill experience is at the Inn at Shaker Village. With more than seventy guest rooms throughout thirteen restored structures, each stay is a unique experience. Rates range from approximately $100 per night for standard rooms to upwards of $160 per night for suites. Make sure to dine on delicious seed-to-table meals from the heirloom garden by candlelight in the Trustee's Office Dining Room.

Scenic Byways of the Bluegrass

Here's the thing about Kentucky: a drive from the easternmost point of the state (Paw Paw, Pike County) to the westernmost point (the Kentucky Bend), following all posted speed limits, will take you almost five hundred miles in roughly eight hours. That's *a lot* of driving. And if you're following your GPS or directions you printed from an online search engine, you're going to miss some of the best parts of the state! If you really wanted to, you could meander your way from Paw Paw to the Kentucky Bend over the course of several days.

For the less fearsome road warrior, the best way to experience the uniqueness and beauty of the state is along the scenic byways that crisscross Kentucky. Here are some of our favorites:

Old Frankfort Pike (Kentucky 1681) has to be near the top of your list; it's internationally recognized as one of the most beautiful drives in the world. Stretching between Lexington and Frankfort, Old Frankfort Pike takes you through the rolling, verdant hills and past some of the world's most illustrious and picturesque horse farms. Cruise along beneath the shade of native tree canopies and make a stop at Wallace Station for a quick bite to eat. This is a drive you won't want to speed through.

Running not quite parallel to Old Frankfort Pike and intersecting it at one point, **Pisgah Pike** (Kentucky 1967) is another essential drive for horse lovers. Pisgah Pike winds past the Versailles Road Castle and WinStar Farm, home to some of the most coveted stallions in the state.

Also nearby is scenic **Midway Road** (U.S. 62), which will take you past Lane's End Farm, a favorite of Queen Elizabeth II when she visits Kentucky.

Head East on Kentucky 32 to see the **Covered Bridges of Flemingsburg**. Three historic bridges dot the landscape around the town: Goddard Bridge, Grange City Covered Bridge, and Ringo's Mill Bridge. Stop at Yoder's Country Market for pie.

A bit farther east, wander down U.S. 23, also known as **Country Music Highway**. The region surrounding the highway has produced a number of stars, including Loretta Lynn, the Judds, and Dwight Yoakam. Maybe there's something in the water?

West of Lexington, winding through the Knobs, is the **Lincoln Heritage Scenic Byway** (U.S. 31 East to U.S. 150). Explore Lincoln's birthplace in Hodgenville, the bourbon distilling industry around Bardstown, and take a moment of serenity at the Trappist monastery at the Abbey of Gethsemani.

⌐ THE ANNUAL GARRARD COUNTY TOBACCO CUTTING CONTEST

Tobacco is one of the most labor-intensive crops and the only crop for which machinery has not yet replaced the hands and backs of laborers. At the end of the summer, tobacco farmers and any help they can find must move through their fields and hand cut the tobacco leaves row by row. Then, they hang it in barns to cure. Kentucky has a rich agricultural tradition, and tobacco has remained one of its primary cash crops for more than a century.

Burley tobacco is a light, air-cured tobacco with tall stalks. Harvesting burley tobacco has traditionally involved an enormous amount of physical labor. A worker on foot will cut each burley stalk close to the ground with a hatchet and then spear four or five stalks on a stick. The loaded stick is later lifted into a curing barn and hung from poles running up and down the barn.

Since 1981, the Garrard County Cooperative Extension Service has helped honor this state tradition by hosting the annual Tobacco Cutting

Tobacco dries in a barn in central Kentucky. The Garrard County Tobacco Cutting Contest honors the labor-intensive tobacco harvesting techniques.

Contest in Lancaster. The community gathers to watch farmers compete in a battle against time and the elements. Because harvesting season comes in late summer, this labor is made even more tiresome by the heavy heat that settles over Kentucky at this time of year. The extremely competitive participants are judged based on their overall time and the number of stalks cut. The grand prize is $500 and a plaque, not to mention some pretty supreme bragging rights.

Visit these sources for additional information on the destinations and topics covered:
- *Kentucky State Parks: parks.ky.gov/parks/recreationparks/old-ky-home*
- *The Kentucky Derby: www.kentuckyderby.com/party/food-and-entertainment/libations*
- *The History Channel: www.history.com/topics/daniel-boone*
- *Kentucky State Capitol: capitol.ky.gov*
- *The Garden Club of Kentucky: gardenclubky.org*
- *Rebecca Ruth Candy Factory: www.rebeccaruth.com*
- *Buffalo Trace: www.buffalotrace.com/distillery*
- *Battle of Perryville: www.battleofperryville.com*
- *Shaker Village of Pleasant Hill: www.shakervillageky.org*

Part IV

NORTHERN KENTUCKY AND THE OHIO RIVER VALLEY

You've probably heard this one before: northern Kentucky is so separate from the rest of Kentucky that it's not really a part of the state! But tell us, why wouldn't you want to claim one of the most haunted places in the world? Or the sisters who wrote the "Happy Birthday to You" song? You'd miss out on Louisville's Mega Cavern, a house that looks like a UFO and most of the cool river towns that sit on the Ohio River.

We want all of Kentucky, and that includes the northern section. We've included the Ohio River Valley as a whole. Did you know that if you jump into the Ohio River in Louisville (not something we actually recommend you do), you'll be treading water in both the widest and deepest section of the river?

17

A ROAD TRIP TO WAVERLY HILLS SANATORIUM

Waverly Hills Sanatorium stands tall and intimidating on top of one of the highest hills overlooking Jefferson County, Kentucky. It is a massive building—180,000 square feet—and foreboding in its darkness and mystery. Think of all of the ghostly adjectives you can; Waverly is all of them—creepy, eerie, spooky, bone-chilling, hair-raising, and on and on.

Whether you believe in the supernatural or not, be fully prepared to be spooked. A tuberculosis hospital where thousands died—some estimates say as many as sixty-four thousand died there before the antibiotic streptomycin was discovered in 1943—and that has been featured on all of the best ghost hunting shows that cable has to offer has to be at least a little frightening. But the tour, while definitely proving to be scary in its own right, is also extremely informative, interesting, and fun.

Now, here's your public service announcement: If you get spooked easily, hate horror films and scary movies, or don't believe in ghosts, this road trip might not be for you. Might not. That's only one possibility; you could also have an absolute blast. You might nearly claw the skin off the arm of your travel companion but that doesn't mean you won't be having fun. A lot of people died while at Waverly Hills. That isn't speculation or folklore or a ghost story; it is a fact. Many tens of thousands of people suffering from tuberculosis in the 1920s and '30s died at this hospital where their friends and families had sent them to get well. So whether you believe in the paranormal, it is hard to think that anywhere in the world has ghosts if this place doesn't.

If you're freaked out at this point, consider that this road trip might not be for you. But if you can go into this experience with an open mind, eyes and ears; listen to what your guide has to tell you; and listen to the history and ghost stories, you'll be just the right amount of scared.

Here are the most important things we learned on our tour:

- Its history. A wooden two-story hospital was originally constructed in 1910, but with tuberculosis rampant in the area, the building wasn't big enough to house all of the patients. So a new building was constructed in 1924 with five floors designed to house five hundred patients—though, in the height of the epidemic, it is believed there were more than one thousand occupied beds at Waverly Hills. The expanded sanatorium opened in 1926 and was its own community. It had its own post office, dentist, and barbershop, and because doctors weren't sure how TB was contracted, once you came to Waverly as a patient or as staff, you weren't permitted to leave until a cure was found. By the 1950s, tuberculosis was nearly eradicated thanks

The body chute—originally built to move heat up to the sanatorium—that was used to move deceased bodies infected with tuberculosis out of Waverly Hills.

to the antibiotic, and the hospital was closed in 1961. It reopened a year later as the Woodhaven Geriatric Center but was closed by the state in 1980 after rumors of patient abuse. Charlie and Tina Mattingly purchased it in 2001 and have opened it up for tours.

- The body chute wasn't originally intended to be for bodies at all. When the building was constructed, architects didn't have a plan for how to heat such a massive space. Doctors didn't want furnaces or broilers on top of the hill because they interfered with the patients' heliotherapy, which was basically fresh air and sunlight. So this tunnel was built to move heat and supplies from the bottom of the hill up to Waverly. But when the TB epidemic reached its height and death counts were high, the tunnel was used to move bodies out of the sanatorium so that the surviving patients wouldn't be able to see how many people were dying.

- Room 502 was actually a washroom where nurses could shower and dress between shifts. This room is one of the most famous at Waverly Hills because it is rumored to be one of the most haunted areas. A young, unmarried nurse committed suicide outside this room after she realized she was pregnant and had contracted tuberculosis. Years later, it is said another nurse killed herself by jumping from the room's window. The guide will tell you that it is common for women to become very nauseous or dizzy when they go inside this room, especially if they are pregnant.

- If you're looking for ghosts, visit the fourth floor. Despite the sickness and death, Waverly Hills was a hopeful place. The sick spent lots of

Room 502 on the fifth floor of Waverly Hills Sanatorium is rumored to be one of the most haunted places inside the hospital. Women often report growing nauseous on entering the room because of its dreadful history.

A ball in the old children's wing of the Waverly Hills Sanatorium in Louisville. Ghost hunters report accounts of child spirits moving this toy around the room.

time together; kids played games on a rooftop swing set. They made the best out of a difficult time. Because of this atmosphere, many of the ghost stories you hear from Waverly are fun and light-hearted ones: kids playing with rubber balls and plastic trucks that people leave for them or a man playing catch with his dog in the hallway. But scarier things have happened on the fourth floor—people have gotten locked into rooms even though there are no locks on the doors; an ice-cold feeling of dread might fill your body for no reason; shadow people appear; lights come from rooms with no electricity; doors slam shut when no one is around them. Even the tour guide said he didn't like the fourth floor. So if you're looking for ghosts on your trip, try starting there.

- There were few reasons to perform autopsies at Waverly. The morgue had only three body coolers because very few bodies were kept for any length of time. Very little was known about TB, and because it was labeled the "White Plague," many people immediately thought of the Black Plague and were afraid to touch the bodies of those who'd died of the disease. In actuality, a person can't contract TB from a dead body, but none of this was known at the time. The bodies moved through the morgue and out of the body chute quickly, where they were claimed by family members or—because many were superstitious about the disease and thought the spirit of the illness would "jump" to them if they were around their deceased loved ones—were placed in a mass grave on the property. Waverly did perform some autopsies because, at the time, a hospital was required by law to conduct autopsies on 17 percent of the dead. An autopsy table, the body coolers and several beds are still in Waverly's morgue. Guests are often invited to lie down on the trays and allow themselves to be enclosed in the body cooler for a few moments.

If you go: Make sure you schedule a tour or book an appointment. There is absolutely no one allowed on the property who is not on a guided tour. The no trespassing regulation is strictly enforced. Go in with an open mind, and be respectful of the other guests in your tour group. Don't tease or taunt or scare. The ghosts believe in payback.

What it costs: The two-hour guided tour is $22 and worth every penny. You'll walk through all five floors of the hospital with an extremely knowledgeable guide and get a lot of history of the building, its former patients and current ghosts. You'll spend about ninety minutes inside the hospital and body chute; the first half hour is devoted to a video about the sanatorium and a few clips from ghost hunting shows it has been featured on. The cost of tours goes up from there. The four-hour (half night) paranormal investigation is $50 and goes from 12:00 a.m. to 4:00 a.m. The eight-hour (full night) tour and paranormal investigation is $100 and goes until 8 a.m. No one under eighteen is allowed on these investigations. These tours are available March through August on Friday and Saturday evenings. Reservations are required. Waverly Hills also offers a few daytime historical tours and private all-night tours. For more information about all tours available, visit the Waverly Hills website at www.therealwaverlyhills.com.

How to get there: Waverly is located at 4400 Paralee Lane in Louisville, but getting there is a little tricky. Get directions to Bobby Nichols Golf Course (4301 East Pages Lane, Louisville). When you turn into the golf course, follow the road around a couple greens and then go left at the fork. Follow that road (which is pretty narrow, dark and winds straight up, up, up) until you break over the top of the hill and pass through the iron gates. You can't miss Waverly Hills towering in front of you.

If you spend the weekend: Be brave enough to book the eight-hour paranormal investigation where you will spend the night in the hospital with a group and look for ghosts. Sleep in the next morning and set out across Louisville to experience some of the great things that Possibility City has to offer!

18

A ROAD TRIP TO LOUISVILLE'S MEGA CAVERN

Mammoth Cave might have cornered the market as the world's longest natural cave system, but the Louisville Mega Cavern gets its big name as one of the largest man-made caverns in the country.

Originally excavated by the Louisville Crushed Stone Company as a massive limestone quarry, the miners blasted out rock for more than forty years to create an expansive, complex system beneath Kentucky's largest city. Realizing the large, yawning rooms blasted out of the mine could be utilized in a variety of moneymaking ways, Louisville Crushed Stone was rechristened as Mega Cavern and began welcoming visitors, businesses and, believe it or not, recyclable waste.

But let's back up a bit. During its heyday in the mid–twentieth century, Louisville Crushed Stone mined limestone for various road construction projects across the country. The cavern's first shift in purpose came during the Cuban Missile Crisis in 1962, when the mine was reserved by the government as a bomb shelter capable of housing up to fifty thousand people. The shelter would have protected mostly military servicemen and their families, but the tour guides like to point out that Colonel Harlan Sanders was on the list too. Maybe, maybe not—we take that with a grain of salt. Either way, the cavern would have made a remarkably safe and comfortable refuge from a missile attack.

Beneath the surface of the earth, it's always a balmy 58 degrees Fahrenheit; the cavern is capable of withstanding a 260-mile-per-hour tornado; and underground water reservoirs would have naturally filtered

Mega Cavern in Louisville is a man-made former mine that now hosts visitors for ziplining, ropes courses, and other tours.

a potentially contaminated water supply. If you weren't driven mad being trapped with 49,999 other people and no sunlight, it might not have been the worst situation had Kennedy's blockade not worked out quite as well.

In the modern era, Mega Cavern boasts more than four million square feet of space spread beneath the Louisville Zoo and Henry Watterson

126

Expressway; it made sense to the owners that the excavated rooms could be used for new, contemporary purposes. The main attractions are the zipline courses that stretch throughout the cavern, some more than seventy feet above the cavern floor; the mega challenge, a sort of nouveau ropes challenge course for all ages; the Tram Tour, a guided history of the cavern, making stops to learn about its potential as a bomb shelter or the worm farm (yum!); and Lights Under Louisville, a mile-long holiday light display that allows tourists to drive their own cars through the cavern to see the decor. We took the tram tour. Our mothers wanted to go ziplining, of course.

Mega Cavern's other modern use is as a home for a diverse collection of businesses. There are storage units, climate-controlled storage rooms, space to bring boats underground during the colder months, and, oddly enough, a thriving recycling initiative.

If you go: You should definitely make a reservation for MegaZips and the MegaChallenge as those are the more popular attractions. You can also make reservations for birthday parties and group events.

What it costs: Prices for MegaZips and MegaChallenge vary across the attractions, days of the week, age groups and time of day. The MegaTram is a standard $13.50 for adults, $12.00 for seniors and $8.00 for children. Lights Under Louisville will run you $25.00 per car, $35.00 per van or $50.00 if you want to take a limo through. A full listing of prices can be found at www.louisvillemegacavern.com.

How to get there: Once you're in Louisville, take the Henry Watterson Expressway to Poplar Level Road. Hang a right on Taylor Road, which will dead end at the entrance to the cavern.

⌐ *BELLE OF LOUISVILLE*

It's one of Kentucky's most iconic landmarks, and it doesn't sit in Kentucky at all. The *Belle of Louisville* is a former passenger ferry and steamboat that moors near Riverfront Plaza in downtown Louisville. It's easy to write the *Belle* off as just another tourist attraction, but aside from sightseeing cruises and occasional steamboat races, the *Belle* has starred in its own fascinating story for more than one hundred years.

The *Belle of Louisville* is a famous riverboat on the Ohio River.

The *Belle of Louisville* travels down the Ohio River. The *Belle* hosts special events and river tours with catering and bar service.

Now the oldest operating river steamboat, it was first launched in 1914 as a ferry between Memphis, Tennessee, and West Memphis, Arkansas. The *Belle* later went on to push oil barges along the Ohio River during World War II and also served as a floating United Service Organizations nightclub. But where the boat really kicks up its heels is the Great Steamboat Race.

Taking place every year on the Wednesday before the Kentucky Derby as part of the Kentucky Derby Festival, the Great Steamboat Race pits the *Belle* against any steamboat challenger brave enough to take it on. The first race was the *Belle*'s first launch after its restoration in the 1960s against the *Delta Queen*. The event was so popular, it is said that more spectators crowded the shores of the river than Churchill Downs for the running of the Derby that year.

If you're down by the river and catch the *Belle* in dock, get a ticket, head to the bar, and raise a toast to the grand old dame who holds court over the Ohio River.

↱ THE HAPPY BIRTHDAY SISTERS

Stick with us for a moment; this story about a joyful, seminal song starts out sad but ends up somewhere happy.

If you walk diagonally across the street from the Frazier History Museum in Louisville toward the I-64 overpass and look down into the

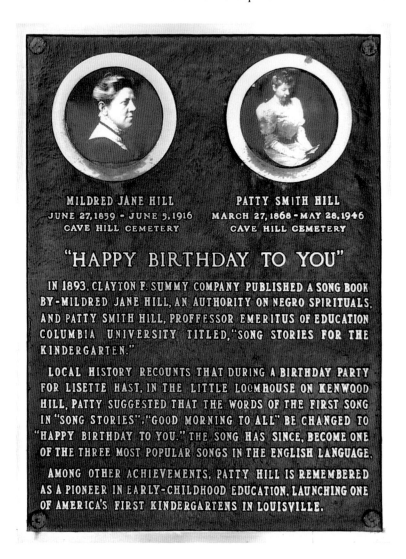

Louisville is home to the sisters who wrote the song, "Happy Birthday to You."

bushes next to a seventeen-space parking lot, you'll find the only current commemoration of Mildred and Patty Hill, teachers and songwriters who penned the song "Good Morning to All." You might know it better as "Happy Birthday to You."

"Good Morning to All" was originally written in 1893 for a songbook called *Song Stories for the Kindergarten*. Both women worked for progressive early education with the Louisville Experimental Kindergarten School. Mildred, the songwriter, wrote the music, and Patty penned the lyrics as a greeting song for her young students. But during a Louisville birthday party, it was suggested that the song be changed to "Happy Birthday to You." And the rest as they say…was not the end of the story.

Copyright claims have persisted for years among various groups seeking royalties for the ubiquitous tune. Most folks agree though: the Hill sisters wrote "Good Morning to All," and that song is the basis for our modern iteration of "Happy Birthday to You."

So why is this small memorial to two influential Louisville educators and the writers of one of the world's most recognizable songs sitting under an interstate overpass next to the "Happy Birthday to You" parking lot? The answer is: hopefully it won't be for much longer.

The Patty Smith and Mildred Jane Hill Happy Birthday Park nonprofit organization has begun raising funds to build a memorial park on a tract of land at the corner of Fourth and Chestnut Streets that pays tribute to the sisters' contributions to both music and education. A far more fitting homage than a small, downtown parking lot.

19

A ROAD TRIP TO BOWMAN FIELD

OK, confession: it's a bit difficult to separate the Art Deco architecture and the romance of flight from the history and reality of Bowman Field. It's not hard to imagine handsome pilots in bomber jackets striding across the tarmac or families waving goodbye and watching planes depart from the administration building.

Though small by comparison to our regional airports today, Bowman Field is part of an essential chapter in aviation history. The first commercial airport in Kentucky, Bowman is also the oldest continuously operating airport in the country.

Founded in Louisville in the 1920s by A.H. Bowman with several partners, Bowman Field was originally the base for one of the earliest aerial photography firms. Soon after opening operations, the 465th Pursuit Squadron (Reserve) brought their planes to the airfield, and a few years later, airmail service began flying between Louisville and Cleveland, with passenger service to follow soon after. Eastern Air Lines, Trans World Airlines, and the original Continental Airlines all operated commercial passenger service out of Bowman Field.

One of our favorite highlights of the airfield's history was the landing of the *Spirit of St. Louis* by Charles Lindbergh in 1927. Approximately ten thousand eager spectators came to see the hero-aviator. Benches had been installed earlier in the decade for locals to come gather and watch the planes take off and land as a form of cheap entertainment.

But it was during World War II that Bowman Field flourished as the busiest airport in the country. A large investment was made to expand

Now primarily used by chartered private planes, Bowman Field in Louisville is noted for its history and Art Deco–style building.

the airfield while thousands of servicemen completed combat-readiness training. When a bomber squadron moved in, Bowman was nicknamed "Air Base City." A large assortment of air force and naval aircraft called the field home.

Even if you haven't been to Bowman Field, you've probably seen it standing in as the base for Pussy Galore's Flying Circus in the James Bond film *Goldfinger* (1964). While you'll never be able to visit the gold depository at Fort Knox, the knowing Bond fan can still walk in Sean Connery's footsteps at Bowman.

When you drive up to Bowman Field, you'll be struck by its beauty, primarily the Art Deco–style administration building that overlooks the runways. Built in 1929 along with the similarly styled Curtiss Flying Service Hangar, the administration building served as the main terminal for flyers, complete with weather service and a restaurant. The other prominent building in the Bowman Field Historic District is the Army Air Corps Hangar, which sits opposite the Curtiss Hangar.

Today, Bowman supports the KY214 Civil Air Patrol, or CAP, as well as several commercial airlines like Central American Airways, Falcon Aviation and Aero Club of Louisville. Almost all government and commercial operations were moved to Standiford Field International Airport on its completion in 1947.

Bowman Field is Kentucky's first commercial airport and the oldest continually operating commercial airport in North America.

You'll want to come for the beautiful Art Deco buildings but stay for the aviation. The airfield averages more than two hundred operations per day, and you'll never get a better view of takeoff and landing than you will from the benches along the fence by the tarmac. While we were there, the security guard on patrol was kind enough to take us up to the domed turret at the top of the administration building where we were able to look out across the full expanse of Bowman Field. If you're not lucky enough to run into an employee, the doors to the terminal are usually unlocked so visitors can explore the historical photos displayed on the walls. You can also make a reservation at Le Relais, an Art Deco–style restaurant inside the terminal. Though it was too cold to use the day that we were there, Le Relais has a large patio overlooking the tarmac and runways.

If you go: Try the doors to the administration building. If they're unlocked, you'll be able to explore more Art Deco details inside along with photos and artifacts from Bowman's storied history. There is an observatory on the top floor offering 360-degree views of the airfield if you can find someone to escort you up there.

What it costs: Nothing. Park your car and feel free to wander around or just hang out on a bench and watch the planes take off and land.

How to get there: It's not hard to spot Bowman Field on Taylorsville Road as soon as you exit off the Henry Watterson Expressway in Louisville.

LOUISVILLE WATER TOWER AND PUMPING STATION

Rising up from the sloping banks of River Road, the Louisville Water Tower and Pumping Station has been an icon for innovation and public works for more than 150 years. The Louisville Water Tower is, in fact, the oldest ornamental water tower in the world. No longer in service, the industrial municipal project disguised as a Greek temple is now home to the WaterWorks Museum.

The Doric-columned water tower began pumping water in 1860 at a rate of more than 12 million gallons per day. The water tower and pumping station have been credited with keeping Louisville cholera-free during the epidemic of 1873.

The Louisville Water Tower and Pumping Station is the oldest ornamental water tower in the world.

Pay a visit to the WaterWorks Museum in the old pumping station to see historic photos and plans for the project as well as film reels that show the water station in action.

KAINTUCKEE PRONUNCIATION GUIDE

Kentuckians sure do have a unique way of pronouncing things, and if you're saying it wrong, that's the quickest, surest way to tell that you aren't a local. Here's a rundown of some of the more commonly mispronounced or misused words:

Louisville: Start with the simpler pronunciation: Loo-uh-vuhl. Then, try it like a native: Luh-ll-vuhl.

Versailles: Ver-sigh is a chateau near Paris; Ver-sales is a town in central Kentucky

Yosemite: Yo-sem-i-tee is a National Park, but Yos-eh-might is in Casey County, Kentucky.

Athens: Sure, you'll visit the Parthenon in Aah-thens, Greece, but you'll find one of the best antique stores in the state in Ay-thens.

Coke: It's always Coke, *never* soda or, God forbid, pop. If you want a Sprite, just say so, or if your host asks if you'd like a Coke, say "Sure! What have you got?"

Y'all: Yankees say "youse guys"; a proper Kentuckian will refer to y'all.

E-I-E-I-Oh: In some parts, a pen might be a "pin," also, you might have "bin" there.

G is for Gone: Some might talk low, some might talk slow, but 'round here, feel free to keep it casual and drop those *g*s. Hey! Where y'all goin'?

THE FIRST CHEESEBURGER

A cheeseburger is a hamburger with cheese added to it. Seems simple enough, right? Well it isn't if you're the one trying to stake claim on crafting the very first cheeseburger ever made. Ever.

Adding cheese to your beef-and-bun combo became popular in the 1930s, and here in Kentucky, every good citizen and burger enthusiast knows that the cheeseburger was invented at Kaelin's Restaurant in Louisville. In 1934, Carl Kaelin threw caution to the wind and placed a piece of American cheese on a hamburger patty in his new restaurant. A culinary treasure was born, and Louisville still claims to be the birthplace of the cheeseburger, and rightfully so.

Restaurants in Pasadena and Los Angeles, California, both claim the rights as their own. Ultimately, in 1935, a trademark for the name "cheeseburger" was awarded to Louis Ballast of the Humpty Dumpty Drive-In in Denver, Colorado. But what's in a name? That's simply a formality.

Today, Kaelin's Restaurant is closed and Kaelin's Coffeehouse now stands in its place. But the legend of the cheeseburger lives on, and with it, a town proud of its claim to culinary fame.

↱ UNITED STATES MARINE HOSPITAL OF LOUISVILLE

Antebellum Louisville was a boomtown with a river-based economy. Shipments traveling up and down the Ohio River to the Mississippi or back up the northeast passed through Louisville on their way. With such a large part of the economy dependent on the boatmen who kept the Louisville economy afloat, then-senator Henry Clay sponsored legislation to create the Louisville Marine Hospital.

Situated on the Ohio River in Louisville's Portland neighborhood, the marine hospital opened its doors to sickness, injuries and all manner

The Louisville Marine Hospital is the only facility built by the Marine Hospital Service that's still standing. It served boatmen who made it their lives' work to keep the Louisville economy afloat.

of ailments. The hospital saw a lot of diseases like cholera and malaria, accidents like boiler explosions and victims of cold and heat exposure.

Since the sailors contributed a nominal share of their paychecks each month toward the upkeep and treatments at the hospital, all manner of workers could receive care, not just the rich and privileged.

During wartimes, the hospital also served wounded servicemen sent to their facility.

The Louisville Marine Hospital is the only facility built by the Marine Hospital Service that's still standing. The building is considered one of the best examples of antebellum architecture in the United States today. Regrettably, there are no tours of the grand old building, though it's very easy to visit the surrounding grounds just off I-64 West, near the Louisville Riverwalk. If you'd like to donate to the Friends of the Marine Hospital, funds are being accepted to assist with future renovation plans.

FAMOUS KENTUCKIANS

Kentucky has so many notable natives that it even has two very famous locals who share the same name. The state is home to two famous Cassius Clays.

The first was born in 1810. He was a newspaper publisher, a naturalist, a politician who fought against slavery, and a talented orator. From 1861 to 1869, the first Cassius Clay was the United States minister to Russia under President Abraham Lincoln. More notably, and perhaps unfortunately, Cassius Marcellus Clay married a fifteen-year-old girl when he was eighty-four.

The second Cassius Clay was born in Louisville in 1942. This guy is a boxer. And not just any boxer, he is the self-proclaimed greatest (and who can argue with that?) who "floats like a butterfly, stings like a bee." He is a man of many accomplishments—Olympic champion, three-time heavyweight champion and orator in his own right. This Cassius Clay changed his name to Muhammad Ali in 1964 to reflect his acceptance of the Muslim faith. He retired from boxing in 1981 but remains one of the most famous people in the sport.

It might seem impossible, but this state's bloodlines get even more famous than that. To start, President Abraham Lincoln, the sixteenth president of the United States, was born in Kentucky. This is a certainty,

Colonel Sanders, who founded Kentucky Fried Chicken, is buried at the Cave Hill Cemetery in Louisville.

no matter what Illinois claims. Colonel Sanders—who basically invented fried chicken—is from Kentucky and built his Kentucky Fried Chicken empire here.

And don't forget Kentucky's royal family, known to commoners outside of the Commonwealth as the Clooneys. Everyone knows George, but he's only one of the famous clan. His aunt, Rosemary, was an incredibly talented singer and actress who starred in *White Christmas* alongside Bing Crosby in 1954.

Talented actress and singer Rosemary Clooney is buried in her hometown of Maysville. Visitors leave pennies on her grave to honor her song "If Teardrops Were Pennies."

This Lifetime Achievement Grammy–winning singer's recordings included the number one hit "This Ole House" and "If Teardrops Were Pennies," a song that inspires visitors to Clooney's grave in her native Maysville to leave pennies on her headstone. George's father, Nick Clooney, is a respected journalist, news anchor, and television host.

Kentucky has birthed a slew of other famous Hollywood faces, including news anchor Diane Sawyer; the incomparable Johnny Depp; Naomi, Wynonna, and Ashley Judd; nearly half of the Backstreet Boys (Brian and Kevin); definitely more than half of the *Hunger Games* main cast (Jennifer Lawrence and Josh Hutcherson); and modern musical groups My Morning Jacket and Nappy Roots.

But perhaps some of the most notable Kentuckians were the authors and scholars like Thomas Merton, Jesse Stuart, and Hunter S. Thompson who published groundbreaking works that have made the state home to innovative ideals throughout its history.

20

A ROAD TRIP TO GENERAL BUTLER STATE PARK

All roads lead somewhere, as do all rivers. The Kentucky River, which starts its course in the Cumberland Mountains, winds its way through the Bluegrass Region before joining up with the Ohio River along the banks of Carrollton in Carroll County. You really get a sense of the power of natural elements when standing at the water's edge and watching eddies swirl and small waves lap at the shoreline. Boats cruise the river, and citizens from Carrollton tend to gather at the waterfront park for a meal, a stroll, or to fish.

High up on a hill just outside Carrollton is the best vista that overlooks the confluence of two major bodies of water. When it's not high summer, you can see through the trees and along the Ohio River as it marks the boundary between Kentucky and Indiana.

The lookout is situated along one of the trails that wind through General Butler State Resort Park. We've always been advocates of the Kentucky State and National Park Systems, and General Butler is no exception. You can stay overnight in the lodge or pitch a tent on the campgrounds, have a meal in the Two Rivers Restaurant, squeeze in a round of golf or a tennis match, lay by the pool or participate in one of the myriad daily activities put on by park staff.

Along with the distinction of sitting at the junction of the Kentucky and Ohio Rivers, General Butler is unique in its additional historic site: the Butler-Turpin State Historic House. To the best of our knowledge, General Butler is the only state resort park to have a historic site on its property as well.

General Butler State Park overlooks Carrollton and the joining of the Kentucky and
Ohio Rivers.

The Kentucky River meets the Ohio River at Carrollton.

The Butler-Turpin House, also known as the William O. Butler House,
and the state park itself are named in honor of General William O. Butler.
A graduate of Transylvania University in Lexington, Butler went on to
make a name for himself as a major general in the United States Army,
as a Democratic congressman, and later as a vice presidential candidate.
During his military service, Butler served in both the War of 1812 and the
Mexican War, where he was second-in-command to Zachary Taylor at the

The Butler-Turpin House at General Butler State Park in Carrollton.

battle of Monterrey, and as commanding general of the United States Army forces in Mexico City after he took over for General Winfield Scott. He left service however, to accept the Democratic vice presidential nomination in 1848 with Lewis Cass as his running mate. Candidates from the Whig Party eventually defeated the two: Zachary Taylor and Millard Fillmore.

Originally built in 1865, the Greek Revival–style home displays furniture, documents and artifacts that tell the story of the family's connection to and impact on Kentucky history along with the contributions of their slaves. If you're planning to stop by the house for a tour, you'll want to call and make a reservation first. Tours are led by appointment only or on limited days and times in late May through early November.

If you go: You'll want to combine an excursion to General Butler State Park and the Butler-Turpin House with an afternoon in Carrollton proper. The quaint town boasts cute cafés and shops as well as an impressive waterfront park.

What it costs: Rooms at the General Butler State Resort Park Lodge average about $100 per night for a standard room or $140 for a cottage. There's also ample camping in the park.

Admission to the Butler-Turpin House is $5 for anyone eighteen or older, $3 for children and teens and free for children under 6 years old.

How to get there: Taking I-71 is the easiest route for those coming across the northern part of the state. Carrollton is almost exactly halfway between Cincinnati and Louisville along the Ohio River. If you're traveling from central or southern Kentucky, you'll want to hook up with U.S. 421 in Frankfort and head north to Carrollton.

THE COVINGTON UFO HOUSE

The next time you're driving south on I-75 crossing over the Ohio River back into Kentucky, take a quick scan of the Covington hillside on your right, and see if you can spot something a little bit different. Warning: this is not recommended if you're actually driving said car.

The UFO House, also known as the Futuro House, is visible from I-75 South as you cross the Ohio River into Kentucky.

146

Particularly on bright, sunny days and especially when the trees aren't quite so loaded down with leaves, you should be able to spot the shining silver surface of Covington's Futuro House.

Actually a prefab house from the mid-twentieth century and not a spacecraft from another world, there were only about one hundred of these so-called Futuro Houses ever manufactured. Much like the kitsch of an Airstream trailer, the Futuro House is a retro remnant of the past.

If you'd like to take a closer look, head up Wright Street in Covington; we guarantee you won't miss it. But be polite, it is a home after all.

Visit these sources for additional information on the destinations and topics covered:
- *Waverly Hills Sanatorium: www.therealwaverlyhills.com*
- *Louisville Mega Cavern: www.louisvillemegacavern.com*
- *Belle of Louisville: www.belleoflouisville.org*
- *Bowman Field: www.flylouisville.com*
- *Abbey of Gethsemani: www.monks.org*
- *Kentucky State Parks: http://parks.ky.gov/parks/resortparks/ general-butler*

Part V
SOUTHEASTERN KENTUCKY AND APPALACHIA

Our final stop on My Old Kentucky Road Trip is to the east into Appalachia and the Eastern Coal Fields. If you're into outdoor adventure, this is the place you want to be. There you'll find the Daniel Boone National Forest, Red River Gorge, and the Appalachian Mountains. Take a drive along the Country Music Highway with Dwight Yoakam blasting from your speakers. Wind your way to Paw Paw; it's as far east as you can go in Kentucky. Or, take a boat down the Big Sandy River, but watch out for any Hatfields and McCoys along the way.

The Appalachian region of Kentucky is the area that is, perhaps, the most steeped in history. It was through the Cumberland Gap and down the Wilderness Road that Daniel Boone made his way into Kaintuckee. Now a national historic park, Cumberland Gap was traversed by the Shawnee and Cherokee tribes long before Boone led groups of settlers through the mountains.

The culture here is colored with coal. Many of the cities and towns in the region were former "company towns," where the coal companies built communities to house, feed and care for employees and their families. The Kentucky way of life is hard to let go, it's something of which we're all fiercely proud.

21

A ROAD TRIP TO NATURAL BRIDGE AND THE RED RIVER GORGE

You have to make the trip to Natural Bridge State Resort Park near Stanton, Kentucky, if only to ride the sky lift. Never mind that this incredible natural sandstone arch spans seventy-eight feet across and bows sixty-five feet above the forest near Red River Gorge. Never mind the natural process of weathering is what created this breathtakingly improbable formation over millions of years. Jump on (literally) an open-air cart and enjoy the unbelievable views around you as this enormous pulley system hauls visitors up and down the mountain. You could always hike to the top on a well-maintained trail and do a little bit of exploring on your own, but getting to relax in your skeletal car as your legs dangle over the deep valley is a much more memorable way to get to the top (you can always hike back down).

Formations like Natural Bridge are some of the great wonders of the world—arches, passageways, and bridges allowed to form in nature without the touch of man over millions of years. More than 2,300 acres of the Daniel Boone National Forest surround the rock arch and make up Natural Bridge State Park. It was founded as a tourist attraction in 1895 and became one of four original state parks. There are over twenty miles of trails to nearby natural formations like White Branch Arch and Henson's Cave Arch.

Natural Bridge stretches across Wolfe and Powell Counties and bumps up against Red River Gorge, a canyon system on the Red River

The skylift at Natural Bridge State Park carrying visitors up to the natural rock formation.

Natural Bridge, a sandstone formation carved over millions of years, near Red River Gorge.

in eastern Kentucky that is a twenty-nine-thousand-acre protected national geological area. People come from miles around to visit this intricate canyon system that features high sandstone cliffs that attract rock climbers from around the world, rock shelters, waterfalls, and even natural bridges. There are more than one hundred natural sandstone arches scattered throughout Red River Gorge, but none are as large and as impressive as Natural Bridge.

Grab your favorite walking shoes and a few friends and take a weekend trip to Natural Bridge. After you've ridden the sky lift up to this wonder of nature, hike down and explore some of the surrounding notable formations located around the bridge's base. Start your day early so you can make your way into the neighboring Red River Gorge to experience some of the most breathtaking views in the state. Give rock climbing a try, or find a quiet spot to read your favorite book. This is a perfect place to soak up the marvelous natural scenery that is so uniquely Kentucky.

If you go: Visit the gorge's website before you head out so you'll know all of the spots you want to see. Red River Gorge is pretty massive, particularly on foot from within its high cliffs, so you want to make sure you have plenty of daylight to hit your favorite peaks. The Natural Bridge website provides a great guide to the various trails throughout the park.

What it costs: Not a thing just to hike around and enjoy the beauty of Natural Bridge or Red River Gorge. There is a small fee to ride the sky lift up to the bridge, but you can pay for one-way tickets or round trip. Make sure you to check the schedule before you go, as the lift does not run year round. In some areas of the gorge, camping fees are imposed.

How to get there: Take Mountain Parkway to Kentucky 11. This highway will take you everywhere you from Natural Bridge State Resort Park past the infamous Miguel's Pizza—where you must stop for an amazing lunch—into Red River Gorge.

> **If you spend the weekend**: The gorge is far too magnificent to stay in just one place all weekend. Grab your tent, a backpack, some snacks, and your favorite hiking boots and hit the trails. Each leads to a more breathtaking view—like Chimney Rock, which isn't far from Natural Bridge—than the one before it.

MOONSHINE

Any liquor that played a direct role in the beginnings of NASCAR is a liquor that you just know is going to have an interesting story.

Moonshine, white lightning, rotgut, whiskey for impatient people—whatever you call it, it has played a huge role in the culture of not just eastern Kentucky, but the entire Bluegrass State. Notoriously strong in alcohol content and illegal for the homebrewer, moonshine's recent increase in popularity has coincided with a boom in the bourbon and whiskey industries.

Here's the deal: moonshine is basically the same thing as whiskey, but it isn't aged in oak barrels. It doesn't soak up the woody flavors or the caramel colors; it just gets the job done. And listen, if someone is bringing a jar of homemade moonshine to your dinner party, you probably shouldn't ask too many questions anyway.

Back during the Prohibition Era, moonshiners and bootleggers would run their goods across the state and up and down the Ohio River. Trying to stay one step ahead of the authorities, bootleggers would modify their vehicles to go faster and outrun any cop who might be in pursuit. The custom of modifying cars for speed continued even after the Twenty-first Amendment was repealed; bootleggers wanted to keep ahead of the taxman. Thus, a sport was born. Many of the early NASCAR drivers were former bootleggers who had, it seemed, been practicing for races their whole lives.

One last fact about moonshine: do you remember in old cartoons, when you'd see a character, maybe a Yosemite Sam type, swigging out of a giant jug with three big X's on the side? That's not a reference to the adult entertainment industry. It means the contents were triple distilled and was also how the drinker knew he had the good 'shine.

22

A ROAD TRIP TO CUMBERLAND FALLS

It's often called the Niagara of the South, and visitors come from miles around for a chance to see its famed moonbow, a treasure that can only be viewed in two places in the entire world. A 125-foot-wide curtain of water, the dramatic Cumberland Falls and its accompanying state park offer visitors an easily-accessible and close-up view of this natural wonder.

Cumberland Falls was established as a state park on August 21, 1931, but its history doesn't begin there. Geologists estimate that the rock that the mighty falls washes over is about 250 million years old. Native Americans lived in this area as early as 10,000 years ago, making their homes along the cliffs that line the Cumberland River, known in early years as the Shawnee River. In more recent times, Dr. Thomas Walker came across the falls during his 1750 exploration of Kentucky and named it after the Duke of Cumberland, a son of King George II of England. The falls changed ownership several times in the centuries following its naming, with owners including Samuel Garland, who intended to build a water mill but instead built a cabin where he resided; Matthew Walton and Adam Shepard, who have the first recorded ownership of the falls in 1800; and Louis and Mary H. Renfro, who bought four hundred acres including the Great Falls of the Cumberland in 1850. The Renfros were the first to construct a place for visitors to stay who wished to fish and enjoy the beauty of the waterfall.

A few owners and the construction of a hotel later, the Kiwanis Club sponsored a trail construction from Corbin to Cumberland Falls in 1927. About two hundred men and women worked for nine weeks to complete the

Cumberland Falls from an observation point at the state park.

task. In the fall of that year, Kentucky native T. Coleman DuPont, for whom today's park lodge is named, offered to buy the falls and surrounding acreage and give it to the Commonwealth as a state park. It took a few years, but on March 10, 1930, the Kentucky legislature voted to accept the land as a state park. The dedication of Cumberland Falls State Park took place on August 21, 1931, and a new highway to the site from Corbin was created that same year. More than 50,000 visitors came to see Cumberland Falls that first year, and according to the visitor's center, now more than 750,000 people visit the falls each year.

Today, paved trails take visitors from viewing points and the top of the falls down to the lower falls (you might get a little bit wet from the mist in the air), where you can stop at several overlooks for great photo opportunities. One of the greatest parts about this state park is that there is so much to see and do. You can camp at one of fifty campsites with electric and water hookups, showers, and a grocery. You can enjoy fishing and rafting in the Cumberland River (safely away from the falls). You can bird watch and even gem mine inside the state park. And if you're into hiking, Cumberland Falls State Park offers many established and well-maintained trails through its surrounding acres, including some to nearby waterfalls.

Strap on your hiking boots and head down the two-and-a-half-mile path to nearby Eagle Falls. The best part of your journey, which involves steep inclines and stairs, is you get to hike along the opposite side of the Cumberland River than what the state park overlooks. So you'll get to see a truly unique view of Cumberland Falls. Be careful if you take this trip after it has rained for a few days. Because of the trail's proximity to the river, you might lose portions of the path to the overflowing banks. Leave your oxen and wagon behind, usually there is a quick detour to get you back on your way.

If you go: Make sure to fully explore the state park and all of its beautiful scenery, which has the benefit of being easily accessible for all ages. Stick around a few extra days and hike the trails to some of the nearby falls like Eagle Falls. The various trails are well maintained and vary in skill level and length. For more information, visit the Cumberland Falls website or ask the friendly front desk clerk at DuPont Lodge. They're always happy to help.

What it costs: The park is free and open to the public every night until midnight. You can park and walk along a few paved trails that take you from the top of the falls to lower scenic overlooks at the base of the falls. If you're interested in staying at DuPont Lodge or its surrounding cabins, prices will vary from seventy dollars per night to a couple hundred per night for the cabins. Fore more information on lodging and pricing, visit parks.ky.gov.

How to get there: Take U.S. 27 to Kentucky 90. The roads are a bit like a round on a Mario Kart track, so be careful. The GPS is likely to not have any luck around this area, but the locals will get you there just fine. Cumberland Falls State Resort Park is located at 7351 Highway 90 in Corbin, Kentucky.

If you spend the weekend: Take a detour down U.S. 27 into Whitley City, which is about fifteen miles back down Kentucky 90 from the falls. Milton's Burger Hut has some of the most delicious food and friendly servers you'll meet. Order some meatloaf, mashed potatoes, green beans, hamburger steak, fries, a buffalo chicken pizza, cauliflower nuggets, and a thirty-two-ounce milkshake. There's even more if you're still hungry after that. Milton's Burger Hut is located at 740 North Highway 27 in Whitley City. When you finish with lunch, take the short trip into Stearns, where you'll find the Big South Fork Scenic Railroad.

 THE MOONBOW

It's a phenomenon you can't see anywhere in the Western Hemisphere, except Cumberland Falls, which makes this worth the road trip without question. The moonbow is a rainbow produced by light reflected off the surface of the moon refracting off of moisture in the atmosphere. Moonbows can only be spotted at a very few locations, including Victoria Falls in Zambia, Africa, which you certainly can not drive to. Even more uncommon than their daytime rainbow counterparts, these natural occurrences are exceptionally rare because so many factors have to occur at the same time to produce a visible moonbow. Cumberland Falls State Park outlines some of the ideal conditions for viewing:

- There must be a bright, nearly full moon (usually two days before or two days after a full moon) and an almost cloudless night.
- Mist must be rising from the waterfall.
- Moonbows will appear white except on cold, crisp nights in the fall and winter when the atmosphere is drier and more clear. Then colors can be seen.
- Water temperature, fog, and wind direction are also factors.

Lot's of stuff to consider right? And there's even more: even if all of the above occurs, you still have to be in the right place at the right time to catch the moonbow. The time to view the moonbow depends on when the moon is high enough to shine over the mountain and into the river gorge. This can be as early as 7:00 p.m. in the winter and as late as 1:00 a.m. in the summer. It's best to see the moonbow if you are standing along the upper outlook areas above the falls, looking down over the falls.

For a full schedule of predicted moonbow dates, visit the Cumberland Falls website at parks/ky.gov/parks/resortparks/cumberland-falls.

⌐ THE IRON FURNACES OF EASTERN KENTUCKY

As railroads began to cross the United States at a rapid pace in the late nineteenth century, demand for iron began to increase. Businessmen hoping to make a fortune speculating iron for the railroads flocked to areas rich in iron ore, like Appalachia.

Iron furnaces sprung up, and communities sprung up around them. Not only could the giant furnaces help produce the kind of iron desired for railroads, but they also helped produce cast-iron commodities for the surrounding neighborhood.

Unfortunately, these freestanding behemoths used up more hardwood from the surrounding forests than was ecologically or economically sustainable. Fortunately, you can still take a drive out to see some of these incredible structures.

Buffalo Iron Furnace at Greenbo Lake. Kentucky has many similar iron furnaces across the state.

The best known of the Kentucky iron furnaces is the Fitchburg Furnace. Roughly thirty miles east of Irvine in Estill County, you'll have to wind your way down Kentucky 213, also known as Furnace Road, just south of Stanton. Make your way as far south as possible, into Daniel Boone National Forest and pick up Kentucky 52 East. Once you've made it over the mountain, you'll make a hard left onto Kentucky 975. The furnace will be on your left. Make sure to talk some time to hike down by the Furnace Fork waterway on the opposite side of the road.

23

A ROAD TRIP TO BIG SOUTH FORK SCENIC RAILROAD

Traveling to Stearns and taking a trip on the Big South Fork Scenic Railroad is the kind of old school road trip that made us want to embark on this project in the first place. We each had vague childhood memories of riding the train, an excitement about going somewhere and learning something new and, of course, joy at being able to spend a perfect fall day in Kentucky.

Getting to Stearns from Lexington is always an easy drive. Passing through Pulaski and Rockcastle Counties helps the time to pass a bit quicker. Or you can take U.S. 27 due south. Once you get to Stearns, the train depot is surrounded by antiques and craft shops, as well as the McCreary County Museum in the old Stearns Coal and Lumber Company corporate headquarters.

Stearns itself has a fascinating history as a "company town." The town rose up as a trade hub for the Stearns Coal and Lumber Company as it prospered in the early twentieth century. The Stearns Company was responsible for bringing the railway through its eighteen coal and lumber camps in the area and for expanding the economy. The company also brought in the world's first electric sawmill for lumber manufacturing.

More than 2,200 employees and their families enjoyed the benefits of working for a large, prosperous business like Stearns during the boom times. The Stearns Company provided municipal services like water and sewage for its employee-residents as well as recreation like a golf course (which is still well-maintained with tee times available today), tennis courts, and a pool hall.

The Big South Fork Scenic Railroad in Stearns takes visitors through part of the Daniel Boone National Forest to old coal mining towns, including Blue Heron Coal Camp.

The railway depot is still painted in the Stearns Company colors, sage and white. Along with exhibits of artifacts and old photos of the company's heyday, a live bluegrass band was entertaining our group of train riders before we embarked.

When it was time to board, we positioned ourselves right at the front of one of the open-air cars, the better to enjoy the foliage and crisp fall air. A certain kind of traveler might balk at the idea of riding in an open-air train carriage, but there are also closed train cars with windows that open halfway. Being on the train is a nostalgic throwback to the joy of childhood when it was exciting to be around something so large and mechanical, and with a powerful whistle, too! We couldn't contain our smiles as the whistle blew on our way into an excavated rock tunnel.

The short-line train, which takes its passengers into Daniel Boone National Forest and along the Big South Fork of the Cumberland River, is actually a diesel engine. Historically, the Stearns Company was using steam power to move goods and people through the camps. The McCreary County Heritage Foundation however, is determined to put a steam engine back on the

The Big South Fork Scenic Railroad stopped at an old coal-mining town on a day tour. Tour reservations are available throughout the year in open-air or covered cars.

tracks. In 2002, the foundation received the generous donation of an American Locomotive Company (ALCO) 0-6-0 Steam Locomotive, which it has been working to restore. If you'd like to contribute to the Steam Locomotive No. 14 Restoration Project, you can do so through the heritage foundation.

The Scenic Railway offers a variety of special excursions and packages (we're dying to go back for the Moonshine Limited, which ends just in time to hop over to Cumberland Falls to see the moonbow), but the most popular is the K&T Special. The fourteen-mile round trip is nothing but gorgeous. On the fall day that we rode, the leaves were at their peak autumn colors, and passengers are treated to views of the Big South Fork of the Cumberland River as the engine chugs along.

You'll pass through several of the smaller coal and lumber camps that used to be operated by the Stearns Company, but your ultimate destination is the Blue Heron Coal Camp. Part of the Big South Fork National River and Recreation Area, you're greeted by rangers from the National Park Service who give you a brief overview of the camp, its highlights and the layout and then turn you loose for a self-guided excursion. Along with exhibits and installations in the depot, you can walk to the original entrance of the coal mine, explore the ghost structures left throughout the camp and listen to oral histories from the miners who used to live and work at Blue Heron.

Our favorite moment came as we were standing in the middle of the trestle bridge where train cars loaded with coal used to dump their loads down into the coal tipple to be sorted. We were standing and chatting with one of the rangers, surrounded by the Daniel Boone National Forest, when a bald eagle came gliding down the waterway and soared above us for some time before he drifted out of sight. Our new ranger friend commented how rare it was to see an eagle. We cursed our lack of telephoto lens.

You'll spend about an hour and a half at the Blue Heron Coal Camp before boarding the train again and heading back up the tracks through the gorge to the Stearns Depot.

If you go: Make a reservation. It's very easy to book tickets online, and there's no guarantee that any will be available for the date and time you show up. Bear in mind that the railroad is only open from April to October. It didn't seem like there would have been any difficulty on the date we went, but that being said, many of their special excursions book up quickly in advance of events. You'll also want to wear good walking shoes. If you want to see most of the Blue Heron Coal Camp, you'll be trekking up hills to get there.

The full excursion takes the better part of an afternoon, and you have several food options. You can pay a little extra on the front end when purchasing your ticket, and a "Coal Miner's Lunch" will be waiting for you at the Blue Heron depot. There's also a concession stand at the coal camp. We grabbed a couple bottles of water and some snacks at the Stearns Depot before we departed and then grabbed dinner at Milton's Burger Hut in Whitley City (get the cauliflower nuggets) after our excursion.

What it costs: For the K&T Special and the Run to the Gorge, their two main excursions, adult tickets were $22.75, seniors $21.25 and children $13. If you want to add on the Coal Miner's Lunch, it will cost an additional $11. Prices for the special excursions vary quite a bit. You'll want to check the website at www.bsfsry.com for dates and details.

How to get there: From central Kentucky, the easiest route is to take U.S. 27 South through Somerset and Whitley City. Turn right onto Kentucky 92 and the Stearns Depot is only about a mile up.

COAL IN KENTUCKY

There are a lot of opinions and politics that surround coal in Kentucky. We're hoping that you won't mind if we take a step back to take a look at the bigger picture of how a natural resource became such an integral part of Appalachian life and culture.

Commercial coal mines have been a part of Kentucky's economy for almost two hundred years. The first commercial coal mine, believe it or not, operated in Muhlenberg County in the Western Coal Field, not the eastern Appalachian region. After coal production in Kentucky nearly died out during the Civil War, the industrialization of the early 1900s revived the coal mines in a big way. As the primary fuel source for growing cities, coal played a major role in massive economic expansion for the region.

Demand for coal only continued to grow as it was increasingly being used to generate electricity and power industrial machines. Later, during World War II, coal production continued to increase. Midway through the twentieth century, mining operations employed almost seventy-six thousand workers throughout the state. It's no wonder that the mines became the center of life and the economy for so many communities.

Today, Kentucky is the third-largest producer of coal in the United States behind Wyoming (number one) and West Virginia (number two),

A re-created entrance to the Blue Heron coal mine, a stop on the Big South Fork Scenic Railroad.

A model of the old Blue Heron coal mine.

but is the second-largest employer of coal workers. As of last year, Kentucky coal operations employed more than 11,500 workers in twenty-seven counties. Recently, Union County in the Western Coal Fields has exceeded Pike County coal output in eastern Kentucky for the first time in more than a century, though the overall amount of coal production is down across the state.

24

A ROAD TRIP TO KENTUCKY'S EASTERNMOST COMMUNITY

If you want to travel to Paw Paw, Kentucky, go ahead and drive to Virginia and make a U-turn, because you're most certainly going to miss it if you're not paying total attention. Paw Paw is a tiny dot on the map in Pike County, an unincorporated community with proud residents that sits right on the Kentucky-Virginia line.

The town is perhaps best known for the most famous vendetta of the southern Appalachians: the Hatfield-McCoy feud. Over the years, this conflict has become overshadowed by exaggeration and myth, embellishing a riff between two families that led to many deaths. Separating fact from fiction can be difficult in this case, but everyone seems to agree that Paw Paw was a hotspot of conflict between these two families as they crossed back and forth between their claimed territories in their respective states.

This leads to the pawpaw tree incident. According to Pikeville–Pike County Tourism, Tolbert, son of Randolph McCoy, exchanged heated words with Ellison Hatfield on Election Day in 1882. As a result of the fight, Tolbert, Pharmer, and Randolph McCoy Jr. stabbed Ellison to death. Later, the three brothers were captured by the Hatfield clan, tied to pawpaw trees and shot in retaliation.

Now, at this point, at least half of you are wondering what in the world a pawpaw tree is. No, it isn't a grandfatherly nickname for your favorite sapling. Pawpaw is a fruit that grows on a pawpaw tree. The fruit has a speckled green skin that hides a tropical-tasting treat. The fruit has a sort of mango-banana-melon flavor and grows throughout Kentucky, most

A grove of pawpaw fruit trees. Paw Paw is a town in the easternmost part of Kentucky named after the fruit.

Pawpaw fruit is a tropical-like fruit that grows on trees throughout Kentucky. The fruit has a mango-pineapple-melon flavor.

abundantly in eastern Kentucky. It is quite famous in history, actually. Thomas Jefferson had pawpaws at Monticello. Lewis and Clark wrote about pawpaw in their journals. And from Michigan to West Virginia, people have named towns and lakes after this fruit. Because it is so soft, pawpaws bruise extremely easily and can't be sold at grocery stores due to their very short shelf life. Kentucky State University houses the United States Department of Agriculture's National Clonal Germplasm Repository—or gene bank, in simple terms—for pawpaw, and the university is performing research on how to increase the shelf life of the fruit. Until then, enjoy pawpaw jelly, jam, and even ice cream—which is amazing.

To be completely honest, while Paw Paw is a unique town–with an interesting history, there is another reason to make this place a stop on your road trip. Here, you'll be standing in the easternmost community in Kentucky. If you can't appreciate the stop for that purpose alone, consider this: in a state that is 40,409 square miles, the easternmost point in Kentucky (Paw Paw) is 543 miles straight across the middle of the state from the westernmost point in Kentucky (Kentucky Bend). It would take you about eight and a half hours to make the trip from one end to the other. Just imagine the miles of adventures that Kentucky has to offer in between. Doesn't that make you itch to get on the road? Happy travels.

If you go: Don't be afraid to ask the locals about the Hatfield-McCoy feud; they know the history better than anyone. More than half the people you'll talk to know or are related to a Hatfield or McCoy. And some of the best stories of the feud are told here.

What it costs: Only gas and food getting there.

How to get there: Take the Mountain Parkway to Prestonsburg and then follow U.S. 23 south to U.S. 119 East at Pikeville. Then take Kentucky 194 to Kimper where you'll pick up Kentucky 632, or Upper Johns Creek Road. You're still not there yet. Appalachia has lots of ups and downs and twists and turns. At Phelps, get back on Kentucky 194 to Rockhouse Fork, where you'll turn left onto Rockhouse Road or Kentucky 2060, which will take you into Paw Paw and then on across the state line into Virginia. (Then comes your U-turn that will welcome you back to Kentucky.)

If you spend the weekend: Take some to explore Appalachia. It represents an incredibly special part of Kentucky's history and culture. There's nowhere else like it in the world.

Visit these sources for additional information on the destinations and topics covered:
- *Kentucky State Parks: parks.ky.gov/parks/resortparks/natural-bridge*
- *Red River Gorge: www.redrivergorge.com*
- *Miguel's Pizza: www.miguelspizza.com*
- *Cumberland Falls History, Kentucky State Parks website: parks.gy.gov/parks/resortparks/cumblerand-falls/history*
- *Big South Fork Scenic Railway: bsfsry.com*
- *Kentucky State University Pawpaw Program: www.pawpaw.kysu.edu*
- *Aubrey, Allison. "The Pawpaw: Foraging for America's Forgotten Fruit." NPR. September 29, 2011.*

INDEX

INDEX

INDEX

ABOUT THE AUTHORS

Blair Thomas Hess is an avid antique collector and chronic hobbyist who stores sweaters and shoes in her oven and once won a sack-the-pig contest at the Trigg County Country Ham Festival. Cameron M. Ludwick is a bookworm, trivia nerd, and former band geek who still relies on the survival skills she learned at Girl  Scout camp to cope with nature. Both are graduates of the University of Kentucky and live in central Kentucky. Together, these friends travel across the Commonwealth, exploring its various wonders and uncovering its best-kept secrets. Follow the adventure at www.myoldkentuckyroadtrip.com.

Twitter: @MyOldKYRoadTrip
Instagram: @myoldkentuckyroadtrip

All photos by Elliott Hess, www.elliotthess.com.